SHADOWLIVING TACTICAL MANUAL

DANIEL SANTIAGO

Black Operations Publications
Minneapolis, MN

Published by Lulu Press
Additional copies may be purchased online at-
http://www.lulu.com/content/2695362
The author can be contacted at-
brimstone999@gmx.com

ISBN-10: 1-43573-450-5
ISBN-13: 978-1-43573-450-0
Library of Congress Control Number: 2008911260
Printed in the United States of America

DISCLAIMER AND WARNING

Neither the author nor the publisher assumes any responsibility for the use or misuse of any information contained herein. All information is presented for educational or entertainment purposes only. Anyone questioning the safety or legality of any activity herein should contact a second professional opinion.

CONTENTS

INTRODUCTION

Shadowliving is the utilizing tactically of any knowledge to reduce dependence upon, to evade, to resist, to defend against, or to sabotage the encroaching oppression of a system of powerful military and industrial corporations working in concert with the state to abuse its citizens and bully the rest of the world. Shadowliving's main strength lies in its defense by invisibility. Anyone can practice shadowliving and most of its practitioners are not outspoken activists but aloof, detached observers that refuse to comply and assimilate.

The information presented here is based on the personal research and real life experiences of myself and others. Many tactics presented here can be applied, altered, and improved upon given the situation and ingenuity of the reader. Likewise, many tactics presented here are legal, some quasi-legal, and some downright very illegal therefore I leave application of them up to the discretion of the reader.

WILDERNESS SURVIVAL

This chapter was written with the ideas of discussing survival for a short term in the wilderness in North America till one could get help and is rescued. It is not meant as a guide for long term survival and "living off the land." So you will find no obscure mountain men techniques such as making fires with bows and drills, making and tanning hides, or making cordage with plant fibers here. Likewise, I've omitted survival skills used in extreme climates like the arctic, the jungle, the desert, or at sea. They go beyond the scope of this chapter; however, they are excellent books written on those subjects if you wish to do further study which I will mention at the end of this chapter.

The most important thing in a survival situation is your attitude, which must be the will to live. The seven deadly enemies of survival are boredom and loneliness, pain, thirst, fatigue, climatic extremes, hunger, and fear. If you are in this situation don't panic, this will only confuse you further. Sit down, relax, and allow yourself to think, then observe your environment and plan on what you must procure in this order- shelter, first aid, fire, water, food, and finally signals.

Unless you are a survival expert it would be foolhardy to venture into any sort of wilderness without some sort of survival kit for emergencies. There are many commercial survival kits on the market but you may find it cheaper and even more effective to simply make your own. It should at minimum contain a means of making emergency shelter, making fire, extra food or a way of getting food, carrying and purifying water, navigation aids, safety tools, and signaling aids. This can all be assembled in a variety of containers including soap dishes, metal Band-Aid cans, metal candy or medicine boxes, shoe polish cans, 35mm film cans, and dental floss containers. A typical survival kit could contain the following-

Tarp or plastic sheeting, poncho, cord, and multi-tool or Swiss army knife with a wood saw (for shelter)

Two lighters, homemade tinder, waterproof matches (water proof by dipping them in paraffin, shellac, or nail polish), and a candle (for fire making)

A full canteen with a cup and iodine tablets (for carrying and purifying water)

Energy food bars, fishing hooks, fishing line, sinkers, and copper snare wire (for getting food)

Map and compass (for navigation)

A first aid kit, a flashlight with duct tape wrapped around the barrel, a signal mirror, and a whistle (for safety and signaling)

Shelter

Shelter is vital for protection from the wind and rain in a temperate climate, in the cold it will need to be enclosed and insulated, and in a warm climate it will need protection from the sun. Staying dry should be a priority, if it's wet and windy you risk getting exposure from the chilling of your body temperature. Exposure is a serious condition and can be even fatal.

The shelter should be near a good signaling site, available water and firewood, and building materials if needed. Certain sites should be avoided- streambeds that can fill up in a flashflood; game trails unless you wish to be awaken by a bear or moose, and marshes where the insects will make nights VERY miserable! Likewise, natural hazards such as dead standing trees, areas of possible rockslides or avalanches, ant nests, and bat caves should be avoided.

If you're lucky you may find a natural shelter like natural rock foundations, rock overhangs, or the undersides of fallen trees. Caves and hollow logs can be used but should be checked first for safety. Check for animals or signs of them like tracks or discarded food. They don't take kindly to people squatting their homes. If you're not too far from civilization you maybe could find a picnic area, freeway bridge, old boxcar, storm drain, a mattress, or old tires.

If you can't find one you'll have to construct one from a framework made from poles, sticks, branches, rocks, or suspension line and then covered with materials like a sheet of plastic or plastic bag, old shower curtain, Tyvek house wrap, cloth or sheets, wooded boxes, plywood, galvanized metal sheets, boughs and broad leaves, grass or sod, snow or sand, or rocks. Some types include a lean to,

A-frame, a snow trench, and a snow cave. The A-frame can be made from one pole and one log or one tree and some line covered with a tarp, a poncho, or vegetation. The lean to can be made with a long branch, two Y-shaped branches hammered into the ground to support the long branch, and covering material. An alternate type can be made by tying a line taut between two trees, dropping tarp over the line, and anchoring the tarp to the ground with line and stakes or rocks. Snow trenches are made by digging a hole big enough for your body and covering the top with tarp or branches. Snow caves are dug in a snow drift with the entrance lower than the cave itself, and then the entrance is blocked with tarp or a pack. After building your shelter you should insulate the shelter with material, such as leaves or springy branches on the floor to prevent heat loss from the ground.

First Aid

In a best scenario situation you will be healthy and be in good physical condition and if so you should do your best to remain so. Being a survivor is bad enough without being a sick or injured one. However, you may get injured or worst be already so. Which is why every survival kit MUST have some sort of first aid kit to deal with medical emergencies, until professional medical help can be reached. At least it should have bandaids, gauze pads, roller gauze, antiseptic towelettes, alcohol pads, antibiotic ointment, and some painkillers like Tylenol or ibuprofen. In addition, you should read about and/ or take classes on basic first aid and CPR. These can be taught by the Red Cross, community colleges, and EMT programs. It is crucial to know how to restore the airway, breathing, and circulation; as well treat major bleeding and prevent shock. All of these untreated can cause death in minutes! Treating burns, fractures and sprains, and heat/ cold emergencies should be known as well. Some excellent books on first aid include The Wilderness First Aid Guide by W. Merry and Mountaineer First Aid by Jan Caroline. If you're interested in serious first aid read Where There Is No Doctor by Werner and Emergency Care in the Streets by Caroline. The former was written for refugee medics and the latter for paramedic training.

Fire

You must have a fire for warmth, cooking, and light at night. A fire also helps to keep wild animals away. The main three ingredients for any fire are tinder, kindling, and fuel. These ingredients should be gathered and added slowly to the fire once it's ignited. The location of the fire should be level, have good air circulation, and be clear of combustibles such as dry leaves and grass. The fire should be built in a pit if possible and definitely be built against logs or rocks to reflect its heat and conserve fuel. Do not build it large- small fires burn better. Remember the old saying- Indian builds small fire, whiteman builds big fire. If you have to build the fire on damp ground or the snow, place a flat stone or parallel logs where it will be built first.

Dry grass, dry moss, dried citrus fruit peels, dead leaves, wood shavings, dry birch and cedar bark, fir cones, dry pine needles, cattail down, thistle, rodent or bird nest lining, bird down, dried evergreen pitch, and the inside tissue of fungi make excellent material to crush into tinder. The tinder should be the size of a grapefruit and can be ignited by match, butane lighter, or a road flare; by focused sunlight from glasses, magnifying glass, binoculars, or camera; or from the sparks of flint and steel (from a welding striker) or touching the terminals of a battery together (a cell phone battery with steel wool or a car battery with jumper cables are great for this). A clear piece of ice shaped like a magnifying glass and polished with body heat can be used to focus sunlight as well. So can a piece of plastic wrap filled with water and twisted into a sphere making a makeshift lens. There's also this product on the market made of a magnesium block with a striker. You scrape off the magnesium, spark the striker, and viola you got fire. Also manmade materials like candles, cotton balls soaked in Vaseline or kerosene, steel wool, dryer lint, wool fibers, charred cotton cloth, newspaper or sawdust mixed with paraffin wax, wax paper, body hair, flattened milk cartons, alcohol wipes, greasy chips (think Fritos), chapstick, gunpowder, sawdust soaked in kerosene or lamp oil, plastic utensils, foam rubber, insect repellant, anti-freeze and calcium carbide (used in mining lamps) mixed with water are good alternatives to natural tinder. Kindling such as dry small twigs and leaves can be added once the tinder starts to burn. Then progress to add larger sticks, branches, and finally logs for fuel. Dry animal dung, dry lichen, dry pitch moss, dried seaweed, oil, animal fat, tires, and upholstery can be used as emergency fuels.

Although they are many more they are four basic types of a fire you can build.

a) Tipi- This is your traditional campfire built in a triangular tipi fashion.

b) Log Cabin- This is good for a lot of heat. First allow the tipi fire to burn to a low flame. Then place four dry logs on the edge of the fire. Allow the logs to catch then add four more logs on the first ones. Repeat until the logs catch and the fire burns strong.

c) Bank- This is a good hasty fire for heating and cooking. It is set against a log with kindling and fuel added at an angle.

d) Star- This is a very economical fire. Arrange the logs in star shape and push those inwards as the logs burn.

Water

In order to live all people require a bare minimum of six pints or three liters of water a day to drink. In a survival situation water takes priority over food. A person can survive for weeks without food, but without water a person will die in five days and in a hot climate even much sooner. If you are short of water limit exertion, rest in the shade, don't overdress, eat only a minimum of food, and whatever you do NEVER drink untreated seawater or urine, blood, alcohol, or smoke tobacco (all of these will increase your thirst).

Water can be obtained generally from surface water in streams, lakes, and springs. Possible water sources are indicated by green vegetation, animal tracks, bee and flies, birds flying in a certain direction at dawn and dusk, frogs at nights, drainage patterns downhill, and human habitation. If you cannot find a reliable water supply it will have to be collected through the rain, dew, vegetation, soil, snow, or condensed seawater or urine. Rain can be collected with a container, raincoat, poncho, or a waterproof sheet stretched taut and pegged down with sticks. Dew can be collected by wrapping a cloth across your legs walking through long, wet grass around dawn to soak the cloth and wring it out in your mouth. If you are near a water source like a river you can dig a hole two to four feet away from it and allow to hole to fill with water, which will be more or less pure. Vegetation can be placed inside a plastic bag, tied shut, and set out in the sun to condense water inside the bag. In dry areas it is possible to build a solar still by digging a hole 3 feet wide and 2 feet deep, put in a container at the bottom, spread a plastic sheet across the hole and hold it in place with rocks, then weigh the center of the sheet with a rock. The water will condense on the sheet and into the container at about a rate of 2 pints a day. In cold climates do not eat snow directly at this will lower body temperature and increase your thirst. Instead, melt the snow with your body heat by placing it in plastic bag and placing it between your layers of clothing NOT next to your skin. Seawater and urine can be treated by placing either in large container and placing an empty smaller container in the center. Then drape a plastic sheet over the large container, tie the sheet down, and place a stone in the sheet's center to weigh it down. In hot climates, cacti can be cut off the top and have the juice sucked up or vines can be cut as high as possibly and its sap UNLESS milky drunken for water..

All water unless collected from rain or condensation MUST be filtered and purified since almost all wild water contains microorganisms like leptospirosis, bilharzia, dysentery, hookworms, or giardia which can make you very sick. Water could be filtered though a sock, bandana, nylon stocking, coffee filter, or a bucket with holes filled with gravel, sand, and burnt wood or charcoal. Then it can be purified by either commercial filter, tincture of iodine (2%), chlorine bleach, or boiling. Commercial filters such as Katadyn, Pur, or MSR can be found in camping and military surplus stores. To purify by boiling simply heat the water to a rolling boil for one minute at sea level and an additional minute for every 1,000 feet above sea level. Tincture of iodine uses 5 drops to 1 quart or liter of water then let water stand for 30 minutes and double the dose if water is cloudy or cold. However, iodine shouldn't be used by children, pregnant women, and those with a thyroid problem. Chlorine uses 2 drops to 1 quart or liter of water then let water stand for 30 minutes and double the dose if the water is cloudy or cold.

Note that iodine or chlorine may not kill cryptosproridium in water; furthermore if you have a suppressed immune system boiling should be the ONLY purification method you use. WARNING- Never gather milky sap from plants, collect water from areas with lots of green algae on the surface, dead animals nearby, near roads, in marshes or swamps, or has a potent smell.

Signaling

When trying to send a distress signal- think THREE. Three of anything- 3 whistle blasts, 3 flashes of a strobe light or flashlight, 3 fires seventy five feet apart in a triangle or a straight line at night, or 3 gunshots. Send your signal, wait a minute, and repeat your signal. Also a mirror, aluminum foil, shiny piece of metal or glass, or a compact disc can be aimed at the sun to flash light to passing aircraft or possible rescuers around as this can be see for miles from the air. Send 3 short flashes, 3 long ones, and 3 short ones again (this spells *** --- --- --- *** also known as 'SOS"). Consider ANYTHING that will attract attention- striking hollow logs, banging metal on wood; laying logs, rocks, broughs, or brightly colored material to say SOS or HELP or V (an international distress signal); making a smoke signal with green leaves/ ferns or damp foliage, burning oil, rubber, or plastic.

Food

Save your energy unless you are experienced do not waste hours of time on complex snares, traps, and nets. As for hunting unless you have a bow and arrow, a firearm, slingshot, bola, or make a spear and are VERY good at it- forget about it! Proficient hunting takes hours of practice; it is best learned BEFORE you really need to do it. Concentrate on edible plants that can be foraged such as grass, inner bark on evergreens, roots and tubers, seeds and grains, cattail, dandelions, fresh seaweed, crabapple, watercress, docks, nettles, and pine needles as well as easy to find animals like fish, frogs (avoid toads), insects unless brightly colored (ants, grasshoppers, locusts, crickets, cicadas, caterpillars, termites, honeybees, and grubs), worms, lizards, turtles, salamanders, bird eggs, and seafood. Simple snares can be made for birds, squirrels, rabbits, hares, opossum, beaver, rodents, dogs, cats, and snakes-

forget about big animals.

When foraging for plants you don't recognize or not listed above use care. Eating the wrong plant can cause sickness or even possible death. The best way is to research edible AND poisonous plant field guides. However- this may not be possible so you may have to apply an edibility test. It's time consuming and you cannot eat anything else during this test but a good way of verifying an unknown plant's edibility. Firstly, reject ANY plant with hairs, thorns, milky or colored sap, shiny leaves, white or yellow berries, umbrella shaped flower clusters, five segmented divisions, red berries or fruit, blackened spurs on grain heads, wilted leaves, or smells like bitter almonds. In addition, reject ALL mushrooms, beans, peas, bulbs, and blue-green algae. Rub some of the plant on your skin and wait fifteen minutes. If you get an itching or burning sensation or get a rash, discard the plant IMMEDIATELY. If you don't, touch some of the plant to your lips and tongue for ten seconds. If the plants burns, stings, numbs, or is bitter discard it. If not, chew and hold it in your mouth for fifteen minutes (do NOT swallow it), spit it out, and wait eight hours. If there are no ill effects such as nausea, stomachache, cramps, vomiting, or diarrhea chew and swallow a spoonful of the plant and wait another eight hours. If you still get no ill effects then eat a cupful and wait another eight hours. If you still feel no ill effects then the plant can be considered safe to eat.

Fishing is probably the most reliable way of gathering food in a survival situation. Almost all freshwater fish are edible and most saltwater fish are edible. Any saltwater fish that is brightly colored or doesn't look like a fish (looks ugly, has ball or box shape, deep-set eyes, parrot beak, prickles, or bony scales) MUST be avoided. Almost all mollusks (mussels, limpets, clams, sea snails, octopus, squid, oysters, sea slugs), crustaceans (crabs, lobster, crayfish, shrimp), and eels are edible. Avoid ANY cone-shaped shell some have a poisonous lethal sting, all jellyfish, and all sea anemones. Sea urchins are edible as well but you must be careful about stepping or brushing against them because of their spines. All sea life in polluted water or during a 'red tide' is best avoided.

The best known way of catching fish is with a hook and line.

It is best time to do this is in the early morning, evening, or before a storm. Although you could get a rod made from a branch then run a line down its length, securing it, then try it at the end, and fish. Fishing with rigs saves time and can be left unattended so you can do other tasks. The easiest is probably a limb line made by tying the line to a strong but flexible line to go two to three feet deep in the water. Tie your baited hook on the line and add a weight six to eight inches above the hook. Bait it in the afternoon and check it in the morning. Another rig called a trotline uses a tree branch or root tied main line about 25 to 150 feet long with up to twenty baited hooks on separate 2 to 3 foot dropper lines. These dropper lines should be spaced 6 feet apart to minimize tangling. Attach the other end of the line to a point across the water or tie it to a rock and drop the rock into deep water. Set it and check it every few hours and let it fish for you overnight.

Another variation of this is to jugfish; using a plastic two-liter soda bottle with the cap on tie a four to ten foot line around the bottle's neck. Then add a weight and a hook a few inches apart to the link. Afterwards, wrap the line around the neck and hold it secure with a rubber band. Bait about twenty of these jugs and cast around dawn and dusk for the best results. A smaller plastic soda bottle (about twenty ounces) can be used for throw lines. Tie a line around the bottle and wrap several feet of line around the container. Add hook, sinker, and bait then sling the line into the water.

Even if you have no fishing tackle with you, it can be always improvised. Lines can be made from electrical wire, cord, or dental floss. Sinkers can be made from a coin, nut, bolt, washer, shell, or rock. Hooks can be improvised with a thorned stem, carved wood, metal cut from a can, a bent nail or needle, a safety pin, wishbone, a bird claw, paper clip, an earring or other piercing jewelry. Corks, 35 mm film cans, pillbottles, small balloons or condoms make good floats. Lures can be used from feathers, aluminum foil, zipper pulls, colored yarn or cloth, buckles, spoons, coins, straw, jewelry, copper tubes, and bullet casings. Find bait like flies, flesh, grubs, worms, minnows, maggots, slugs, crickets, corn, small fruit, pieces of meat, cheese or bread from your surroundings.

Other methods of fishing include spearing using a harpoon made with poles and lashing. It is best done in shallow water with lots of fish. To make the spear, sharpen a straight branch then lash two separate sticks to both sides of the spear. Afterwards, wedge the two sticks apart with another straight stick. Then go to the water, watch for a catch, and spear it quickly. The side sticks will close, trapping the fish. Sometimes, this works better at night if you have a flashlight which can be used to lure them to the surface of the water.

With lots of patience and luck you can try catching the fish with your hands. Lower slowly your hands in the water. Allow the fish to come near, grab it by the gills, lift it out and throw it on the shore. You could improvise a seine by taking a t-shirt tying it to two sticks then stretching the shirt you can scoop fish from the water. Other methods using elaborate nets and traps are not usually worth the trouble and shooting and throwing grenades in the water are just plain impractical. When was the last time you were in the woods and a case of grenades just happened to be near by!

Warning: All fish that have slimy gills or eyes, flabby flesh, a bad odor, or flesh the stays indented after being pressed MUST be discarded.

Small game can be trapped with either snares or deadfalls. Birds can be trapped by baiting fruit with fishhooks or pieces of wire that will catch in their throats when eaten. A good snare can be made with light and flexible copper or piano wire, electrical wire, cord, fishing line, leather or nylon bootlaces, or white or green dental floss. These should be made of a loop a fist wide, four fingers above the ground, and a hand width from the nearest obstruction on the trail. But commercial snares made from self-locking stainless steel aircraft cable from trapping stores are better. All are usually positioned on runs with lots of tracks, feeding areas, den openings, logs, water sources, dug up foliage and ground, flattened grass, signs of droppings, natural bridges, or fresh carcasses. Birds can be snared by suspending a line of snares across a stream above water level. Be prepared to make at least twenty snares spread out over a square mile per catch. Avoid disturbing the environment, don't tread on the trail, and don't spit or urinate near traps. Before setting the snare rub dirt on your hands and after setting rub it with mud, ashes, food, or smoke it to mask your scent. Check the snares at least twice a day, preferably before sunset and after sunrise. After capture- kill the animal as humanely as possible as it will try to bite you.

All food must be prepared properly and cooked before eating to avoid illness from parasites. Plants usually require little preparation, just wash and boil them in water. However, animals must be skinned, bled, and gutted before cooking. Fish should be cleaned by cutting the throat to bleed, scaling from tail to head, gutting by inserting a knifepoint into the anus and cutting open the belly to remove all organs and gills, and roasted immediately after. Mollusks and crustaceans are boiled alive for at least ten minutes. Small game is skinned by hanging upside down with the legs apart, cutting along the legs and pulling the skin off or by making a slit across its back and pulling off the skin in opposite directions. They are then gutted by opening the abdominal cavity carefully to avoid rupturing internal organs then rolling out the organs and intestines. The blood and organs such as the liver, kidney, and heart of small game should be saved as it is rich in nutrients. Birds should have the head and feet removed, plucked, gutted, and then boiled in their skin. Reptiles are just beheaded and gutted since they can be roasted in their skins. Turtles- are a special case- they should be boiled until the shell is loose and the removed before cooking. Frogs and salamanders just have to be skinned and boiled. Insects should have all legs, hairs, and wings removed before being boiled or roasted. The two simplest ways food can be cooked is by either boiling in a tin can or metal box of water or skewing it through a stick and roasting it over a fire. They are many more ways such as wrapping food in non-poisonous green leaves and burying it in ashes under hot coals for baking or if you have fat frying food on a flat rock or sheet of metal heated by placing next to or on top of a fire. However, more elaborate techniques such as making Dutch ovens are too time intensive for our purposes.

All food gathered, cooked, but not eaten should be preserved immediately as plants will lose their nutrition and fresh meat will outright spoil in all but the coldest climates. Drying and smoking are two good ways of preservation in a wilderness setting. To sundry it must be hot, dry, and sunny then cut off all fat from the meat and slice it an eighth to quarter-inch thick and a half-inch to one inch wide. Thread the meat on poles so they don't touch another and hang it above at least one foot above a non-resinous wood (NEVER use evergreen wood) fire till the surface is dry then hang it in the sun to dry until the meat will snap when bent. The meat will now keep indefinitely. To smoke make a rack from greenwood around a slow fire. The fire shouldn't be big or hot, just make good smoke. Cut fat away from the meat then cut into thin slices. Lay the meat over the rack and cover the rack with cloth or boughs. Smoke the meat overnight or till dry. The meat should look dark and brittle. Cutting up the food, boiling it, and putting it a solution of salt water strong enough to float a potato can also preserve it. As well as pickling the food by covering it in a mixture of two parts juice from a lime or lemon with one part of water.

Sources for further study of wilderness survival-

Tom Brown's Field Guide to Wilderness Survival, by Tom Brown,Jr.
Best of Woodsmoke, by Richard L. Jamison
Primitive Outdoors Skills, by Richard L. Jamison
Outdoor Survival Skills, by Larry Olsen
Survival Skills of the Native American Indians, by Peter Goodchild
Wildwood Wisdom, by Ellisworth Jaeger

SELF-DEFENSE

It is vital that everyone knows how to defend him or herself against a violent encounter. In an ideal world this wouldn't be necessary but it isn't. Humanity sad to say can be species capable of horrifying acts of cruelty towards its fellow members. It goes from dictators who abuse their authority murdering in the millions sometimes to serial killers who rape and kill for a depraved thrill.

Years ago I published a zine called "Angel of Death" which documented the astonishing methods a human's life could be taken. Some people (some of questionable mental stability) found the zine entertaining while many others (like my own mother) found it disturbing and practically unreadable. But, one thing for sure it opened my eyes to the incredible amount of evil another person is capable of.

It is for this reason alone a study in self-defense can literally save your life. I'm not to scare the reader but the threat is very real. I personally have been robbed four times- twice at gunpoint, once by strong-arm, and another being bludgeoned with a hammer! Luckily for me, my assailant was a brainless crackhead who had limited knowledge of human anatomy and even less of physics. I also know friends who were assaulted, women friends who were raped, friends who were stabbed by their own girlfriends, and people who were stabbed to death over stupid drunken arguments. Having belonged to a subculture, which contains individuals whom can be extremely violent, I've probably witnessed more violence than a person whom lives a mainstream 'normal' life. However, self-defense is for EVERYONE.

Situational Awareness

A very wise man once said 90 percent of self-defense is not being in stupid places, doing stupid things, or being around stupid people. You want to avoid trouble in the first place and the best way to do that is to be aware of your environment. Many times you can spot trouble before it comes. Use the color of readiness as used by the military, law enforcement, and martial artists. Code White means a total state of unawareness, oblivious to one's surroundings.

Unfortunately, many people walk through life in this exact state. Code Yellow is a state of alertness and one is attentive to their surroundings. Code Orange is a state of alarm when one detects a potential threat and the mind is preparing for an attack. In other words, it's when one gets the feeling that 'shit is about to hit the fan.' Natural flight or fight reflexes are triggered and adrenaline is dumped into one's system. Code Red is the state when an attack is underway. If you are in Code Red you are in combat!!! When in public always try to stay in code yellow as attackers target people who seem unaware, preoccupied, or easily surprised.

To get a better understanding of this go to a public hangout like a mall or shopping center for a half an hour and watch people. Try to observe who's in code white or yellow; don't expect to see much code yellow or red. Better yet, go to a 'rough' neighborhood if you want to see all four in action. Observe everyone's demeanors and emotional states then try thinking like a mugger or a rapist. Who looks like an 'easy' victim? Who seems like one who can 'hold their own.' Finally, who seems like one 'you wouldn't want fuck with.'

When in code yellow, know your environment. If you don't know it talk to the locals, look at the neighborhood, read the graffiti if you can, and notice how the homes look. Stay alert- scan the area for possible 'troublemakers.' Think about hypothetical hostile scenarios that could arise. Watch for ambush zones like behind trees, utility boxes, ATM's, shrubs, corners, dumpsters, cars, walls, rooftops, construction sites, tunnels, alleys, and bridges. Learn to use windows and other reflections to notice possible threats. When walking the streets avoid listening to a Walkman or iPod because they make you deaf to your surroundings. If a building looks like trouble take the stairs not the elevators. Be cautious in public restrooms; use a stall if possible instead of the urinal. Alter your travel route and pattern in your routine. Use caution in parking lots, bars, nightclubs, parties, rest stops, liquor stores, late night convenience stores, amusement parks, carnivals, and red light districts.

If you expect to go into 'hostile territory' expect the unexpected, try to blend with the locals, don't flaunt wealth (lots of money or expensive jewelry), go with friends if possible, and carry a weapon. Wear clothes you can fight and move fast in such as loose fitting pants, sneakers, or boots. Tight skirts and high-heeled shoes are a liability. Consider making a 'decoy wallet' with a couple of one's wrapped in play money. If you get robbed you can drop the decoy and run. Above all, trust your intuition (aka-sixth sense) usually if the situation feels bad it probably is.

If you sense danger you're in Code Orange and you will have seconds to determine if the threat is dangerous. Survey the area 360 degrees and do a quick 'threat analysis'. What's his behavior and emotional state (look drunk, look crazy, etc.)? What's his intent (robbery, picking a fight, or just 'talking shit')? His range (close enough to pull a weapon)? His positioning (to the front, side, or rear)? If you have a weapon, get it ready and look for escape routes. Watch his hands which may be holding or hiding a weapon. Watch for potential weapons nearby that you could use or he could use. Watch for any 'help' or silent partners that might come to his aid. Watch your footing for ice, sand, or oil. Tripping and falling is not only embarrassing it can be dangerous as well. Likewise, you may be able to use any loose footing to trip him up. Look for potential cover like desks, doors, cars, trees, fences, walls, dumpsters, heavy machinery; and potential escape routes like doors, windows, staircases, and fire escapes.

If you reach Code Red try to maneuver to the side or rear of your attacker, as this will make fewer targets for him. Use psychological distractions like acting 'crazy', pointing away from you, eye feints or talking to an imaginary friend to make him think someone's behind him, or feigning surrender when preparing to attack. As well as physical distractions like throwing dirt, salt, sand, objects, or using pepper spray. Use surprise, give no warning. Assume your attacker is armed and never fight unarmed by choice (if you don't have a weapon <u>find</u> one fast). If the attacker is has a weapon or 'help', you are in a kill or be killed situation- go ballistic! Use every dirty trick in the book including lethal force. Bite and scratch him, gouge out eyes, pull hair, stomp on toes, pull a 'Tyson' (bite ears and nose), and rip out earrings and piercings. If you can escape get somewhere well lit and crowded. Knock shit over as you're running like trashcans, signs, and newspaper boxes. Try to attract attention by throwing something through a window as this may trip an alarm.

Tactical Mindset

When faced with a potential violent situation you can comply, escape, defuse, or fight. How you will respond will depend on the situation. Complying with an attacker may be necessary if you are surprised or facing a superior force. If you're unarmed and robbed at gunpoint you'll have no choice but to comply and give them your wallet. Trying to fight in this situation can get you killed. Escape should be your first priority. There's nothing cowardly about fleeing a dangerous situation that can get you seriously injured or killed if you have the chance. Defusing a hostile person by using psychology and reasoning skills is an important art to know. You'd be surprised how many assaults and homicides begin over petty arguments. If you can talk an intoxicated or high person out of violence you've won! In many martial arts they teach 'victory without violence' is the highest principle. Fighting should be the last resort but if you've to fight because of facing deadly force, surprise, or a rape situation commit totally do everything you can to incapacitate and if necessary kill your attacker. However, violence is no game- if can escape or defuse the danger- do it!

Conflict Defusing

If a potential attacker is at a distance, unarmed, drunk, angry, or just talking 'shit' you may be able to defuse him. Keep your distance hopefully out of an attack range; make no physical contact whatsoever- it could be mistaken as hostile. Keep your cool and try to control your emotions. Don't take it personally if the person says something insulting. Use a poker face, as your body language and voice should be non-threatening, confident, and assertive. Choose your words carefully, words can be weapons- in some areas blood is the price for using 'fighting words.' Be especially cautious if you're dealing with someone from a different cultural or socioeconomic background, if you can't back it up with fists- don't say it! Be relaxed but alert- use the Code Orange mindset so you have a tactical edge if the situation turns violent. Keep your hands up and open to protect your vital targets, watch his hands closely, and NEVER turn your back on him.

Hand-to-Hand Combat

Ok- so you gave the thug your wallet but he has 'other ideas' (especially if you're female), the drunken idiot won't listen to reason and tried to take a swing at you, or you met a brawler who insists on 'kicking your ass'. There's an old saying that 'diplomacy is the art, of saying 'nice doggie' till you can find a rock.' Well, this is the 'rock' part! How you will attack should depend on the range of your attacker. The furthest out you can kick. Next closest you can use finger jabs, palm heels, knife hands, hooks, upper cuts, and hammer fists. Finally, more closely you can headbutt, bite, gouge, claw, crush, stomp, and use elbow and knee attacks.

Use a 45 degree angle stance to minimize exposing your vital points, set up your natural weapons, and angle your chin slightly down. If you're right-handed lead your attacks with your left leg. Always stay mobile and balanced, move in quick steps to advance, go back, or to sidestep. Your goal is to use maximum strength of your natural body weapons against his vital points and to destroy his balance while keeping yours. These actions must be automatic, aggressive, and done without hesitation. When you strike yelling and exhaling is important- it focuses you and distracts him. It should be loud and fearful- like a wild animal. All this takes practice- work on accuracy first then speed and power. Practicing in different environments like low-light, nighttime, heat, rain, wind, fog, snow, ice, sand, wet grass, or in confined spaces (elevator, restroom, stairs, hallway, or a car) is important. If you want to get extreme try places like in the water, mud, a hill, or a ditch. You probably won't have the luxury of fighting in a bright warm spacious house when attacked.

Natural body weapons include the head, teeth, elbows, fists, palms, web and edge of the hands (also called knife hands), fingers, knees, shins, instep, heel of the foot, and the ball of the foot. Anything hard should go bone and anything soft to tissue. Let's go into more detail-

Head- You can give headbutts to the nose or jaw.

Teeth- You can bite the nose, ears, throat, fingers, and lips. This should be used only as a last resort because of the danger of possibly contracting blood-borne pathogens such as HIV or hepatitis.

Elbows- You can deliver strikes to the nose, temple, chin, back of the neck, throat, solar plexus, and the ribs.

Fists- Using a lead straight (like a jab but with more power), hook, rear cross, uppercut, shovel hook, hammer fist, or back fist punch you can attack the temple, eyes, nose, chin, back of the neck, throat, collarbone, solar plexus, ribs, kidneys, and groin.

Heel of the palm- You can strike the nose and chin.

Web of the hand- You can grip the neck around the throat.

Edge of the hand- You can whip it to his nose, side of the neck, and throat.

Fingers- Very versatile! You can claw and gouge the eyes, crush the windpipe, twist the ears and nose, stick them in his nostrils then rip them out, and pull hair. Rip out earrings or facial jewelry. Grab and crush the testicles or other soft tissues. In fact, if he is fat then just grab a handful of flesh and tear it apart.

Knees- Deliver strikes to the ribs, solar plexus, stomach, thigh, face, and groin. Plus you can drop your knees on him in a ground attack.

Shins- Attack the thighs, knees, groin, and instep.

Instep- Side kick the knee, groin, or the pelvis like kicking a door open.

Heel of the foot- Kick the knee, shin, thighs, and ribs. Stomp on the toes. If he's on the ground- stomp on his head, neck, ribs, spine, kidneys, and knees.

Ball of the foot - Kick the groin, thigh, knee, and shin.

Vital points which strikes can cause pain and if forceful enough injury or death include the eyes, ears, temple, nose, chin, back of the neck, throat, collarbone, ribs, solar plexus, lower spine, kidneys, groin, thighs, knees, shin, fingers, insteps, and the toes.

Eyes- Very sensitive; scrape, poke, gouge, or throw blinding agents (dirt, salt, bleach) in these. Forceful strikes can cause temporary or permanent blindness.

Ears- This is a special target; a forceful blow with cupped

hands can cause pain.

Temple- This is the weakest part of the skull and a lethal target.

Nose- It stands out and is easy to hit making it an excellent head butt or palm heel target.

Chin- It is best hit with an uppercut at a 45-degree angle.

Back of the neck- Hitting here is known as a 'Rabbit Punch.' Because of its poorly protected this is a lethal target and even a moderate blow can cause whiplash and concussion.

Throat- This target is lethal as well. The windpipe is poorly protected and crushing it forcefully enough can cause hemorrhaging. About an inch to the sides of it runs major blood vessels and nerve clusters that if constricted will cause unconsciousness. It is a perfect target to chop, grab, punch, and squeeze at. .

Collarbone- A good target for a downward hammer fist strike.

Ribs- Strikes are best directed at the lower or floating ribs. If you can get your fingers beneath them they can actually be ripped away from their tendons! This target can be lethal if a rib is broken and forced into a lung or the liver.

Solar plexus- This target has lots of nerves, best hit with an upper cut with the knuckles out.

Lower Spine- A good kick here can immobilize.

Kidney- Although difficult to hit from the front a forceful hit can cause rupture and shock.

Groin- As any guy knows a strike, grabbing, or twisting here causes extreme pain 'nuff said!!

Thighs- The best spot here is on the side about a couple inches above the knee or a forceful strike to the middle of the inner thigh. A good kick to both areas can immobilize.

Knees- Hit with enough force ligaments could be torn and the knee dislocated.

Shin- This target is very sensitive and a powerful kick could fracture it.

Fingers- These could be jammed, sprained, broken, and bitten.

Instep- This area has many small bones that could be broken with a forceful stomp.

Toes- This is the same as the instep. Avoid this target if the attacker is wearing hard leather boots.

To defend against attacks use slips, parries, and blocks. Use slipping to avoid a straight attack and just twist your head and torso left or right. Parrying is a quick, forcefully slap using the palm of your hand to redirect the blow. Blocking is used against circular attacks using your arms, elbows, or legs. Arm blocks intercept overhead, head, and torso attacks by making contact with them with your mid-forearm. Elbow blocks intercept uppercuts and hook punches to the torso by dropping the elbow close to your body and twisting away from the attack. Legs blows intercept kicks to the legs or groin by raising your lead leg up and making contact with the blow with your calves. Following a defense always counterattack afterwards. By choice, NEVER block with your body against an armed attacker. If you don't have a choice then make sure you block the limb holding the weapon NOT the weapon itself. That little mistake costed me a broken hand many years ago.

Knowledge of countermoves against grabs, locks, and strangles is probably the most important defensive aspect of self-defense. This is because these moves are encountered many times in ambushes which you may be taken completely by surprise. You must be prepared to instantly break the grip before a hold takes place especially if your attacker larger or stronger than you. Fortunately, most countermoves do not require much strength (although it definitely helps) but they must be done immediately, hard, and fast keeping up the pressure until the hold is broken. If someone tries to grab your wrists perform a thumb break by twisting towards their thumb and jerking your arm away. If the situation is serious enough you can grab their little finger and break it. If your attacker tries a takedown you can use the inside bone of your forearm as a lever against his nose and eyes or just knee them in the face. Throws can be countered by relaxing, making the attacker support ALL your weight, and grabbing onto them by the pants or belt. If they try to throw you, they'll have to throw themselves as well- which is impossible. A frontal bear hug if they are inept enough to grab you under your arms thereby leaving your hands free can be broken by cupping your hands and slapping their ears HARD or punching their chin, nose, or eyes. Use elbow strikes to their body, hand strikes to their face, and kicks to their shins or groin if the underarm bear hug is from behind. If the frontal bear hug is over your arms break it by head butting them, stomping on their feet, kicking their shins, or smashing your knee in their groin. If they attempt an arm lock distract them by pretending you're in a lot more pain than you really are. Then with your free limbs break their nose, poke their eyes, tear their ears, stomp their instep, use backward elbow strikes, and low backward kicks. Rear headlocks can be countered by a eye gouge, smash to the groin, grinding a one-knuckled fist into their spine or kidneys and then attacking the throat. A side headlock can be broken by getting your hand up into their face from behind their shoulder while jerking their head back and attacking the groin with the other hand and then follow up with rear elbow and hand strikes. Strangleholds are the most dangerous of all holds, which is why it's banned for use by most police departments. To break these you MUST first lessen the pressure on your neck or you can blackout from the loss of air or blood to the brain. This can be done by turning your face into the crook of his elbow, striking the groin and grabbing their right wrist then pulling their arm away. Then afterwards break their little fingers, attack their eyes, ears, throat, groin, or whatever. Go crazy as anyone using a stranglehold intentionally or not is trying to KILL you.

To end up on the ground is probably one of the most dangerous positions to be in. If you happen to be in this position- you must counterattack and get up ASAP!! First, use one limb to block any attack. Then, simultaneously fill your other hand with any weapon available (a rock, sand, dirt, a stick, etc.). Kick at your attacker at his knees, lower body, shin, and groin. Use the other foot to try to pull and lock his legs under him. Get up ASAP!

To defend against multiple attackers seek try to escape, find a weapon, and keep moving. Never allow yourself to be surrounded or cornered. If escape is impossible you must initiate the fight. Attack the immediate threat first being either the best armed, the closest, the one blocking escape, or 'the leader'- in that order. Then hold that person to use his body as a shield against the others, while simultaneously attacking his eyes and throat to take him out of action. Repeat until you can escape. Stay on feet at all times as you do NOT want to go on the ground in this situation. If you do you probably will be seriously injured or even killed from being stomped into the pavement; or as the skinheads like to affectionately call it being boot partied.

If the attacker has a blunt weapon try to find a better weapon and run to get out of range cutting to your left or right. If this is impossible and you're unarmed wait till they swing and the blow has passed you; then close with the attacker and strike. Sounds easy don't it- it is NOT and must be practiced to be even halfway effective. Knife and firearm defenses are discussed later on. Unarmed disarms against an armed attacker unless you're trained or have no choice is a fool's game. It may work great for Jackie Chan or Steven Seagal but they're actors and street fights don't have scripts or retakes. In the movies fights are dragged out for five to ten minutes on the street most fights are over in less than a minute. If you can run and get the fuck out of there- DO IT!!

You must develop speed, power, and timing for these strikes to be most effective. Relax, focus, and execute the blow as quickly as possible. Put your entire body into the blow. Don't attack him, attack <u>through</u> him!! Also your attacker shouldn't be able to see the blow coming. This is known as 'telegraphing' and best avoided by keeping a poker face. Shadow fighting in front of a full-length mirror is ok but the best way to practice is by delivering strikes on a heavy bag or better sparring with a partner so your timing improves and you can put your attacks, defenses, and counters together into one form. In a fight you will not have time to think, all actions must be automatic. Try to drill at least three times a week developing attack combinations (about four strikes at once- for example a front kick, rear palm heel, rear knee, then an eye gouge). Execute a bunch for 3-4 minutes, rest 30 seconds, and then repeat 5-10 times. Also try to stay in good physical condition. Do a battery of sit-ups, push-ups, pull-ups, and some aerobic exercises (running, jogging, cycling, swimming) several times a week- even if just taking a walk instead of taking the bus or driving. If you are overweight or out of shape, your ability to defend yourself will be disadvantaged.

If you carry a weapon-whether it be pepper spray, baton, knife, Maglite flashlight, stun gun, or just a lock and chain 'smiley' (many streetpunks carry these and I've seem them do mucho damage) train with it several hours a month. Learn about several good strikes and practice them. For example, with the baton one is the slashing strike like swinging a bat. A second is the jab in which you whip forward, impact with the target, and retract back. Then a downward circular strike in which move your baton downward then quickly outward in a circle. And finally there is the thrust in which the baton follows a similar line as an uppercut punch or hook punch from the side. Your targets with these strikes should include the hands, wrists, elbows, knees, thighs, solar plexus, ribs, kidneys, spine, collarbone, throat, back of the neck, head, and face. Concentrate on developing speed, power, and accuracy. Train for low light conditions. Learn the disadvantages of your weapons. For example, pepper spray cannot be used in strong wind or in confined spaces. Neither are they as effective in the rain or humid weather and anyone drunk, drugged, or deranged may not even be affected. Do not warn your attacker that you are armed and follow your defense with a counterattack (such as a kick to the knee or groin). Above all, keep it with you at all times. A weapon left in the car or at home is no good in the street.

A word about legalities here you should only use the force needed to stop an attack, escape and then get help or medical treatment if necessary. Anything beyond and it's not self-defense anymore and opens you to criminal felony charges from assault up to even murder. Use common sense when employing these techniques. If someone is being drunk and stupid at a gathering is unarmed it probably isn't necessary to crush his windpipe. A quick strike to the nose and solar plexus will probably do. However, on the other side of the coin if someone insists on beating you within an inch of your life do whatever it takes to survive.

Edged Weapons

This weapon has been around for thousands of years yet it still causes a horrifying amount of deaths each years. The knife is a very mobile and dangerous instrument in the right hands. Respect it and don't underestimate it ever! From an attacker's point of view they have the advantage over guns that they are silent, don't jam, don't need reloading, and are easier to conceal. Most knife attacks are sneak attacks. They are the most effective and most experienced knife fighters will use them! Anyone dumb enough to flash a blade is for the most part either incompetent or bluffing. They mean mainly to threaten not attack. However, this does NOT make them harmless.

If you're confronted with a knife and if you can do it-RUN. Get the fuck out of there!! Anyone within 21 feet of you with a knife is a deadly danger, as this distance can be closed within two seconds. If this is impossible find something to block or fight with. If you have a knife or gun, use it. If you have nothing use something like a coat or jacket (preferably a leather one), backpack, briefcase, stick, table, a chair, or trash can lid to block with. You want to create distance and use barriers like couches, large tables, cars, tall fences, or park benches. Stay mobile, quick, and balanced. Position your body so your vital areas are protected and focus on the knife at all times.

You could 'try' to disarm him. This is NOT recommended and should only be done as a last resort. Forget about that bullshit in the movies. It is very unrealistic and very dangerous. Don't believe me? Have a friend hold a red marker, then try to stab you while you try to 'disarm' him. You will soon find red marks all over you. If those marks were knife slashes and stabs, you'd be dead. If you want to practice have your opponent try to 'stab' you with a plastic knife. Then try to low kick the shin or knees. Grab the knife hand and do not let go. Redirect the knife away from you while closing with your opponent. Then try to knock him off balance and take him down with any attack available (knee to the groin, headbutt to the nose, etc.).

If you decide to carry a knife get one with a serrated blade (which cuts two to three times deeper than a regular blade). It should be good for slashing and stabbing plus fit comfortably in your hand. It should be small and light enough to conceal but large enough to slash arteries and stab organs. A four-inch blade tactical folder with a rubberized grip is a good choice. Avoid switchblades, stilettos, and folding non-locking blades as these are too unreliable. Always keep it sharp and practice with it often. Learn not just slashing and stabbing but also chopping, snapcuts, whipping, and raking. And lastly, never pull a knife unless you plan on using it- it is a lethal weapon.

If you're confronted with a knife and you decide to knifefight (and only goddess knows why you would want to) you will likely be cut at least once. There's an old saying about knife fights- the winner goes to the emergency room and then to jail, the loser gets put in a body bag and goes to the morgue. You want to create movement and distance so you can evade his attacks and advance to launch your own attacks. Use you non-knife hand as a guard for your stomach and throat, a parry, a distraction, and to create openings for your attacks. Regardless of what you see in the movies NEVER throw a knife. Lastly, do not lose your knife- if you do you will likely lose your life.

Your main targets should be his knife hand, the stomach, the groin, armpits, muscle groups that immobilize limbs, and arteries that bleed profusely. Cutting the knifehand will hopefully make him drop the knife and hopefully you can end this bloody nonsense without anyone getting killed. Not only is killing many times unnecessary but it could open up a legal can of worms for you. Remember, you may have to explain this shit to the police and if they're witnesses it will be even worse. Stabbing and then slashing the stomach or the groin will create great shock but death is unlikely unless major organs or the aorta (main artery) are hit. Slashing muscle groups such as the deltoideus (side of the upper arm), triceps (back of the arm), forearm, back of the hand, knee, and the popliteal (back of lower leg) will make that limb useless.

The ugly business of arteries and 'quick kills' deserve special mention. The carotid artery located in the neck can severed by slashing or stabbing one and a half inches deep. This'll cause unconsciousness in five seconds and death in two minutes. The radial and ulnar arteries located on the wrists can be severed by slashing the wrist a quarter inch deep. This will cause unconsciousness in thirty seconds and death in two minutes. The brachial artery located above the elbow inside the upper arm can be severed by slashing a half-inch deep. This will cause unconsciousness in fifteen seconds and death in one and a half minutes. The femoral artery located inside the upper leg near the groin could be severed by stabbing two to three inches deep and twisting the blade.

Quick kills are mentioned only if you are in a desperate situation of having an attacker who is not only bleeding like a stuck pig but just won't go down and keeps attacking!! Sadly, you'll have to take this guy out and fast. Knife thrusts to any of these targets- under the chin, below the adam's apple, beneath the ear, under the rib cage to the heart, the kidneys, the temple, through the eyes into the brain, and the base of the skull will produce death quickly. Now, that I've probably caused you to lose your dinner let's move on to less bloody topics.

Firearms

Before getting a gun-do some serious soul searching because even though a firearm is a great tool for protection not everyone should get a gun. In the wrong hands it becomes a menace. Ask yourself some questions. Do you have a bad temper? Do you drink often to excess? Do you use mood-altering drugs? Do you get depressed often? Do you have children? Are you clumsy or disorganized? If you answered yes to any of these questions getting a gun can well make you a danger to yourself and others. To emphasize this I'm going to tell you a real life experience living in New York. We were partying and drinking in my room I had in a squat. I got my SKS rifle and pointed it at my friend's head as a joke. He told me to check the chamber. I was convinced it was empty and told him so. He told me to check it again and I told him it was empty again. He told me to check it again and finally I checked it. A fucking round flew out the chamber!!! That stunt I pulled was the ultimate in stupidity!! If I pulled the trigger my friend would probably be dead and I'd be in prison for manslaughter. Don't imitate my stupidity at that moment- learn from it as I did. Burn these safety rules into your mind. Always assume the gun is loaded. Point the muzzle in a safe direction. Know what's behind your target. Never put your finger on the trigger until you're ready to shoot. Never pull a gun on someone unless you intend to use it. Never bluff using a gun on someone- this deadly serious business not a poker game. Alcohol or drugs and guns NEVER mix. Take a firearms safety course. Train and practice with it often so you learn to shoot fast and accurate. Keep your gun cleaned and maintained, so it shoots when you need it to. When the gun isn't in use get a gun box or trigger lock to secure it (especially if children are around). Always approach guns with intelligence and respect. Take this seriously- possession of a gun is the possession of the power of life and death over another human being. On the other hand, a gun is a great equalizer. It can give a trained person who is very frail, elderly, handicapped, or female the power of a small army and most criminals respect the deadly power of a gun. As exemplified by a tee shirt I saw a lady in New York wear several years ago saying 'You can't rape a .38'.

The first type of guns I'm going to discuss are handguns that come in basically in two kinds revolvers and semi-automatics. Revolvers have the advantage of being easy to maintain, easy to load, and they almost never jam. Unfortunately, they hold less ammunition (5 to 9 rounds), take longer to load, and can be harder to conceal. A good choice if you're of average build is a .38 special, double action revolver with a 3-inch barrel. If you're of larger build get a .357 magnum. Get a .44 or .45 only if you can handle it, as this is 'too much gun' for many people to shoot accurately. Avoid .22, .25, and .32 calibers, as they don't have enough stopping power. Likewise single action revolvers should be avoided because you have to cock the hammer before firing which will slow you down. Also make sure it has a spur-less hammer because the spurs can catch on clothing (usually at the worst possible moment). Good brands and models of revolvers are Colt (Cobra, Detective Special, Police Positive, Agent, Diamondback, and Peacekeeper), Smith and Wesson (models 10, 60, 64, 67, 586, 686), Ruger SP-101 and GP100, Taurus (models 62, 80, 82, 85, 627), Charter Arms .38, EAA Windicator, and Rossi (models 68, 851, 951, 971). Semi-automatics have the advantage of being able to be located quickly by changing magazines and can hold more ammunition (9 to 18 rounds). However, unlike revolvers they require more maintenance because of the higher amount of moving parts that are prone to breakage. A .380 or 9mm with a 4-inch barrel is a good choice, although .40, 10 mm, and .45 calibers are popular as well. As with revolvers you should avoid calibers smaller than .380. Avoid cheap 'Saturday Night Special' type handguns such as Jennings, Davis, Sundance, Phoenix Arms, Lorcin, and Bryco because of common problems like ammo not feeding correctly and parts breakage after firing as few as 100 rounds. These are problems you DON'T need in a combat situation. They are some decent budget semi autos on the market such as the Star Model B, the Hungarian FEG PA-63 and PJK-9HP, CZ-52 Tokarev, the Russian Makarov (my personal favorite), the Polish P-64 and P-83, Ballester-Molina 45, Llama Minimax, Kel-Tec P11, Firestorm, and Bersa 380. If your budget allows good semi-autos in the $300-$600 price range include the Beretta 92, Ruger P89 and P93, Astra M-4000 Falcon, Glock 17 and 19, Czech 75 and 85, MAB PA15, Steyr GB, Sig-Sauer p220 series, Taurus PT92, Browning p-35, Smith and Wesson (models 39, 59, 908, and 3913), Star Firestar, Walther PPK (James Bond's gun), Springfield Armory P9, and Kahr K9.

When buying a handgun it's a good idea to buy one from gun shows, swap meets, classified ads, from a friend, or other private party as no record is made of the purchase. Get one that is easy to clean, operate, and comfortable in your hand. Prior to buying- inspect it for rust or cracks, dry fire it to check the trigger action, and shine a pen light down the barrel. The barrel should be shiny and smooth with no pits, scratches, or other crap inside. If you buy it used, have it checked by a gunsmith to make sure it's functional and safe. Many retired cop guns make good used gun buys because they're usually well maintained and have no hard usage just some cosmetic wear. Try to get a handgun in blued steel instead of stainless steel because it will be harder for an intruder to spot you in low-light conditions. Buy a good holster for it, preferably nylon instead of leather that will allow you to carry it around comfortably. Buy speedloaders or spare magazines so you can carry and load spare ammunition quickly. Buy a guncleaning kit, oil, and bore cleaner for good maintenance. Load your handgun with good defense loads like Remington (Golden Sabers), Federal (Hydra Shock or Personal Defense), Winchester (Black Talons or Silver Tips), Speer (Gold Dot), Cor-Bon JHP (jacketed hollow point), or Glaser Safety Slugs. But practice with solid point (ball) ammunition because it's cheaper. Learn how to clean and disassemble the gun. Practice dry firing it inside your home aiming, shooting from cover, and getting a good trigger pull. Finally, practice live fire shooting it often at least 100-200 rounds to get a feel for the recoil and to become accurate. Then at least every month practice at least 50 rounds from different stances standing with both hands gripping, one handed grip (with each hand), kneeling, sitting, prone, back on the ground, and behind cover. You never know what position you'll be in if you must use your handgun. Some people paint a luminous line on top of the barrel and white dots on the sights to improve accuracy.

The next type of firearm I'm going to discuss are shotguns. Shotguns make excellent home defense. The first is that it's easy to hit your target at close range. Plus, they are less likely to over penetrate to the next room; a dangerous problem if you happen to like in an apartment or a house with cheap walls. The second, its reputation- criminals respect the devastating power of a shotgun and know a shotgun blast hit usually guarantees death. Many times simply racking the shotgun will have criminals running faster than the Starship Enterprise doing warp 10! Many people have a problem with the recoil, which is why you must brace yourself when firing. Also, more important get the right gauge for your size. If you're small frame get a 20 gauge or if you're large frame get a 12 gauge. Good shells for defense are #2 and #4 shots and for longer ranges (+50 yards) use 00 buckshot and slugs. Folding stocks are good for shooting in tight areas. Pumps and double barrels are good types to buy. Avoid automatics because they need more maintenance and some shells won't feed into them. Good quality shotguns on the market include Mossberg 500, Remington 870, and Winchester 1300. A good idea after buying your shotgun is to attach a mirror to the stock of the shotgun so if you have to look for an intruder you can look around corners and tight spots safely without exposing your head.

When shooting don't move the barrel or you'll misalign your target and miss. I know it sounds obvious but it's a common mistake beginners make. Learning how to shoot at night is important too as if you must use a gun on someone; it's likely to be at night. If you shoot at night don't look at the muzzle blast or you'll ruin your night vision. Count your shots and don't wait till you're empty to reload, do it before that. Shoot to stop not to wound; aim and use a double tap shot- one in the body, one in the head. Avoid what I call Hollywood training, some of those gimmicks shown on TV and the movies will get you shot FAST! Learn the difference between concealment and cover. Concealment like a large bush, tall grass, trashcans, wooden fences, some walls (like sheetrock), and most doors will keep you from being seen but will NOT stop bullets. Learn how to take cover which will stop bullets too like a large tree, a big rock or log, a ditch, engine block of a vehicle, concrete wall, building corner, or heavy furniture. If you can't take cover, drop down and reduce yourself to the smallest mass you can. Stay down, use shadows to your advantage, don't silhouette or skyline yourself, avoid reflections (mirrors, glasses), and use extreme caution with doors, windows, hallways, and stairwells (aka- fatal funnels) as these are VERY dangerous. Take a quick peek below eye level and move to a covered position fast. Don't just think about shooting; think about getting shot too. If you do get shot, keep shooting and don't stop. Most gunshot wounds don't result in death. Then as soon as possible, treat bleeding, shock, and get medical attention.

After buying your firearm and feeling comfortable with it you should make a tactical plan of your living space. Know the layout and note entrances, escape routes, and ambush zones. Have a room where you can make a stand in case of an intrusion. In case of intrusion, lock the door in that room and stay in away from the door. If the intruder attempts to enter-first, warn him once you have a gun, take cover, and aim. Then if he persists and forces his way in shoot him.

If you must hold the intruder at gunpoint maintain complete control. Do not allow him to get in grabbing distance of your weapon. Keep him as far away from you as possible and in an uncomfortable position. Loudly command him to turn around with his hands up, drop to his knees, and lie down spread-eagled. Do not search him. Keep him in this position until help arrives. Warn him that if he makes any slight move he will be shot. Watch him at ALL times while keeping the gun aimed at the center of his mass.

A word about disarming someone who has a gun on you; unless you're certain the gunman will kill you don't even attempt it. This isn't Hollywood, it is VERY dangerous. Besides if he's over ten feet away you're better off trying to escape. If you must try to disarm someone as a last resort, verbally distract him then reposition your body so it's out of the line of fire. After, redirect and grab the gun's barrel or slide then attack him with everything you have.

Legally in general you can use lethal force to defend yourself or others against a lethal threat or to stop a violent felony (homicide, rape, armed robbery, assault with deadly weapon) in progress. You cannot use lethal force to stop fleeing criminals unless they're armed, killed, or severely injured someone. You cannot use lethal force to prevent unarmed criminals from engaging in theft or vandalism or to threaten people threatening you verbally or engaging in non-violent crimes. These are only guidelines. Self-defense laws vary widely from state to state and city to city, from fairly loose to very strict. Case in point, in Texas you probably could 'bend' the guidelines a bit, however in New York City if you break any of these guidelines you will do jail time.

Improvised Weapons

How many times have you watched a horror movie where a terrified woman is running away or hiding from a homicidal maniac? Now look at everything around her and try to spot how many of these things could be used as a weapon. Unfortunately, she usually never uses any of them (if she did the movie would be over in five minutes!) and just meekly awaits her demise. However, this need not be case- in any given home, car, or public place there are dozens of objects that can be converted into self-defense weapons which in the following listing I cataloged 175 (count 'em) commonplace objects. Interestingly, the most dangerously armed places in the home are the kitchen (lots of knives) and the garage (lots of potential bludgeons). Keep in mind that I define an improvised weapon as anything that will distract or hurt your aggressor long enough (a few seconds to a half minute in most cases) to either 1) escape and get help or 2) find a bigger or better weapon to finish them off.

ALARM CLOCK- Swing by the power cord at the head and face
ASHES- Throw into the eyes
ASHTRAY- Smash at the temple, nose, throat, wrists, and base of skull
AXE/ HATCHET- Strike at the side and back of skull, backbone, above hips, and solar plexus
BACKPACK- If it has heavy objects inside swing it at them in their head

BARBED WIRE- Use as a garrote or rope around the arms or legs tightly
BARSTOOL- Pick it up and ram them legs first or hit them on the head again legs first
BASEBALL- Throw at enemy or smash vital areas
BASEBALL BAT- Spin it at enemy's shins or sling at vital areas
BELT- Whip at the temples, jaw, chin, nose, neck, kidneys, and floating ribs
BEER CAN- If unopened, shake it up and pop the top in the face. Then rip can in the half and jab them in their face
BICYCLE- Pick it up by center of handlebars and back of seat. Turn it around fully and fling it, sprocket first in the face. Afterwards, deliver a kick in the groin.
BICYCLE CHAIN- Whip it as a flail striking at vital areas
BICYCLE PUMP - Use it as a nightstick or pour bleach into the pump and blow it in the face after hitting them
BLEACH- Throw some in their eyes and nose
BLENDER- Remove the blades from the blender and use it to slash them
BOILING WATER- Throw it in the face them hit them with the pot
BONE- If it's the turkey, cattle-sized or bigger use as a club
BOOKS- Use large, hardcover flat books as a shield against knife and fist attacks or deliver blows to arms, neck, collarbone, head, and face.
BOOM BOX- Hit them in the head, face, solar plexus with it. Also makes a good shield against a knife
BOTTLE- Club opponent in the head or face or break it and stab him
BRIEFCASE-Whack them on the head with it. It also makes a good shield against knife attacks. Also one ingenious person whom was mugged at gunpoint before decided to put a sheet of steel cut to the briefcase's size inside. He was mugged again, the gunman fired but the victim used the briefcase as a shield and stopped the bullets.
BRICK- Tie a rope around the brick and swing it at them. Can also be thrown or smashed on the head.
BROOM- Use it like a bayonet, thrust handle portion into solar plexus, throat, and deflect knife attacks. Also straw end could be set on fire and jammed into the face.
BUTTOCKS- If held from behind, bend down, jerk their ankle up, and spill them on their back. Then violently drop your weight on

their chest, ass first of course.
CAMERA-Strike them in the head with the lens portion or if it has a huge zoom lens use it as a club.
CANDLE- Any candle 10" or larger makes a good club.
CANDLEHOLDER- As anyone who's played the boardgame 'Clue' can attest, it makes a good club.
CANE- A cane with a hooked handle can be used to beat the skull and hook the ankle, neck, or groin.
CANNED FOOD- Put the can inside a bag, sack, or sock. Tie the bag closed and use it as a club.
CARABINER- Use it a you would brass knuckles. Aim for the nose, jaw, ears, and hands.
CASE OF BEER- This one's from personal experience. After buying a case of beer, some stranger gave us a ride then pulled a knife on us. I beat him senseless in the head with the unopened case. A 24 pack of brews also makes a good shield against fist and knife attacks.
CAR CIGARETTE LIGHTER- Push it in, wait till hot, and burn them with it.
CAT- If it's not declawed throw the cat in their face (the cat will instinctingly grab on their face with ten nice sharp claws) and then kick them in the groin.
CB RADIO MICROPHONE- Swing it at vital areas or use it as a garrote
CHAIN- Fold it double and swing it like a flail
CHICKEN BONE- I read before how a dry drumstick bone broken in two and jagged can make a weapon only to dismiss it as bullshit. Then I read a true story about an inmate in Riker's Island injuring a guard with one. I guess it isn't bullshit!
CHAIR- Thrust chair legs into groin or solar plexus or it as a shield against a knife.
CIGAR- If lit burn cigar into any exposed skin especially the face, necks, hands, or groin.
CLEANER- Throw the Comet or Ajax cleaner in the eyes.
CLEAVER- Grab a nice big one and chop away at their face, throat, arms, hands, and legs.
CLOTHESLINE- Use as a garrote to choke them.
CLOTHESPIN- Pinch at the nose, ears, fingers, genitals, or breasts.
COAT- Use it as a shield against knife, club, or chain attacks.
COFFEE- Throw the hot coffee in their face first then smash them

in the temple or solar plexus with the mug.

COMB- Use a steel rat-tail comb and use the teeth to slash the face or the tail to stab the throat or face.

CORKSCREW- Grab, aim for the face or neck and twist hard pretending you're opening a bottle of fine wine.

CREDIT CARD- A credit card cut in two diangularly and sharpened can be used to strike the eyes.

CROWBAR- Strike with the claw size at the temple, face, throat, and hands.

CURLING IRON- Clench it in your hand and drive it into their face, neck, solar plexus, and groin.

DARTS- Throw at them or clench in your fist and punch away.

DEODORANT SPRAY- Spray in their eyes or put a lighter in front to make a flamethrower.

DIRT- Throw it in their eyes

DIVING KNIFE- Use blade to chop, stab, or slash and club them with the handle

DRAIN CLEANER- Throw it in there eyes, nose, or mouth.

DRAWER- Fling it at them like a frisbee.

DRINKING GLASS- Use the bottom to hit them in the nose, teeth, jaw, collarbone, and temple.

DRILL-Drill at their face, eyes, neck, ear canals, hand, and groin.

DUMBBELL WEIGHT- Thread some cloth through the hole and use it as a club.

ELECTRIC FAN- If plugged in, direct at the face, fingers, or groin. Also can be used as shield against knives and clubs.

ENEMA SYRINGE- Ram it up his nose or ear canal.

EXTENSION CORD- Use it as a garrote or to electrify metal objects.

EYEGLASSES- Fold them up in your fist and use them like brass knuckles, use corners to strike temples.

FACE TOWEL-Tie a bar of soap inside it and use it as a club.

FAN BELT- Whip it at his head, face, hands, and chest.

FILE- A needlepoint file can used to pierce the eyes, throat, neck, solar plexus, under the chin, or up the nostrils.

FILLETING KNIFE- Slash at the hands, wrists, face, and neck.

FILM CANS- The 35mm film size can be filled with and carry all sorts of substances to blind or distract your attacker like salt, cayenne pepper, ash, sand, iron fillings, ground glass, pumice, lye, or caustic potash.

FINGERNAILS- Claw at the face and neck or gouge at eyes and throat.
FIRE EXTINGUISHER- Discharge it in his face or use it as a smoke screen. To make a spear gun with a carbon dioxide extinguisher, stick a sharp rod in the tube and discharge it. Extinguishers also make a great club.
FISHHOOK- Hook into and tear at any exposed skin especially face, neck, and hands.
FLARE- Light it and thrust it towards his face, any exposed skin, or groin.
FLASHLIGHT-Use the big D-cell flashlights as a club.
FLASHLIGHT BATTERIES- Fill a sock with D-cell batteries and use it as a club.
FOOD TRAY- Like the ones you see in fast food places. Slam them in the nose, jaw, or throat. It also makes a good shield against a fist or a knife.
FORK- Stab at the face, neck, solar plexus, hands, and groin.
FROZEN FOOD- Frozen food is usually hard as a rock. In a real life case a man was bludgeoned with 10 pounds of frozen salami producing a wound requiring 55 stitches. Similarly, at a barbecue we observed someone getting slugged with a frozen T-bone steak which cost him a couple of teeth.
GARBAGE CAN LID- Use it a shield against attacks or throw it like a frisbee against their shins.
GLASS- Take a 3 inch wide shard, wrap the hilt with cloth and stab them under the jaw.
GLOVES- Fill it with rocks, gravel, sand, or pennies and slug them with it.
GOLF CLUB- Use it as a club stupid!
GUITAR- Use it a club or take out strings and strangle them with the strings.
HAIRBRUSH- Rake bristles across their eyes. Use the sides to strike the heck and temples. Hammer at the skull and ribs with the handle.
HAIR DRYER- Use it as a club.
HAIR SPRAY- See Deodorant Spray
HAMMER- Use it as a club, except strike claws first. This delivers more pounds per square inch of pressure resulting in greater damage.
HARD HAT- Use it as a shield or strike him with the visor.

HATPIN- Shove it in his eyes or ear canal.
HEAT GUN- If it's on, direct towards any exposed skin or hair then hit them with gun.
HELMENT- Smash them in the head, nose, or jaw with it.
HOE- Lunge into their throat or stomach.
HOSE- Use it as a whip or if it has a nozzle a flail.
HOT SOUP OR HOT COOKING OIL- Throw the liquid in their face then smash them in the head or face with the pot or pan.
HUBCAP- Use it a shield or smash it flat on their head.
ICESCRAPER- Clench it in your hand and slash at their head, face, neck, and hands.
IRONING BOARD- Use it as a shield against attacks or ram them in the chest with it.
ICEPICK- Stab them in the eyes, top of skull, throat, or kidneys. Also can be rammed up their noses or ear canal.
INSECTICIDE- Spray it in their eyes, nose, and mouth.
IRON- If its hot makes a good shield. If cool give a blow to the head with point or swing it by the cord.
JACK- Use it as a club; swing at the head, chest, kneecaps, and neck.
KEYS- Slip it between your fingers and jab it in their eyes and face.
KNITTING NEEDLES- Jab at their face, hands, and chest.
LAMP- While keeping the lamp plugged in charge at them bulb first.
LAPTOP COMPUTER- Hit them in the head, face, or solar plexus with it. Also makes a good shield against knife attacks.
LIGHT BULB- Clasp in hand and hit them in the face with it.
LIGHTER FLUID- Squirt it on their skin and clothes then throw lit flame on them. Also if you're really want make an intimidating effect place the fluid in your mouth and blow it out at them while holding a lighter a foot in front of your face (a.k.a.- fire breathing).
LUG WRENCH- Throw it at them or bludgeon their head with it.
LUMBER- A good 2x4 always makes a neat bludegeon.
MAGIC MARKER- If it's the Magnum 44 type, use it as a fistload and punch away.
MEAT HOOK- This is a terrifying weapon to be faced with as a friend of mine can attest to. It can cause some VERY nasty lacerations. Swing and aim to hook in the face, head, neck, limbs, stomach, and groin.
MICROPHONE- Swing by the cord at the head or face, then choke

them with the cord. If the mike has a stand, even better use it as a staff. At show for a late rock musician known as GG Allin I personally saw a "fan" get his face bludgeoned with a mike stand.
MIRROR- Use the face mirror as a club.
MOUTHWASH- Gargle some and spit it in their face then hit them with the bottle.
MULTI-TOOL- Don't laugh at or underestimate these ever!! I personally know a friend whose brother was killed with one of these. It can also be a multi-weapon! To make a blackjack drop it in a glove or sock and bash away. To make a metal bludgeon open both handles with the pliers down. If it has two knives (probably one regular and one serrated) open and lock both blades to make a double-edged knife. A double bladed knife can be made opening both handles and both knives. The pliers can also be used to pinch, twist, and tear targets like fingers, lips, nose, ears, armpits, and testicles.
NAILPULLER- Strike at the temple, face, neck, solar plexus, and groin.
NEWSPAPER- Roll it up, swat at incoming punches and jab with ends in groin, ears, eyes, throat, and solar plexus. Also newspaper could be rolled, flexed and held like brass knuckles to strengthen punches.
OVEN CLEANER- Spray it on their skin, eyes, and face.
PADLOCK- Clasp in a fist and use as brass knuckles or even more lethal attach a rope or chain to the lock and swing at their head, face, and hands. A padlock and chain is a street gutter punk favorite. Also known as "Smileys", why it's called that I have no idea. I have seen these in action cause serious injury and if you ever get hit with one you will NOT be smiling!
PAINT- Spray Krylon or throw a bucket full in the face.
PEN- Jab at eyes, throat, ear canals, temple, under chin, base of skull, solar plexus, hands, and groin. Pencils and penlights can be used the same way.
PEPPER- Sling it in their face then hammer the head with the shaker.
PICTURE FRAME- Slam it on his head or throw it.
PILLOW- Use it to block a knife or fist attack.
PING PONG PADDLE- Deliver a chop to the neck, head, and collarbone with the edge.
PISS- You could piss in a cup and throw in his eyes or piss in a

bottle and throw it at him. Also there's the favorite of NYC squatters- a big bucket of weeks old piss!
PLIERS- Pinch and crush the lips, nose, balls, or the windpipe (this can kill!)
POKER- Use it a club striking the head and limbs. Can also be used as a bayonet.
POOL BALL- Throw them at their face.
POOL CUE- Use as lance, heavy end first. Ram into stomach, solar plexus then swing at head and ribs.
PURSE- Load with heavy objects and swing like a mace or use to block attacks.
RAKE- Swing at the face
RAZOR BLADE- Slash at face, wrist, and neck.
ROCKS- See Bricks
ROLLING PIN- Makes a great club, ask any pissed off housewife.
RUG- Use it like the coat before mentioned or pull a Tom and Jerry, jerk it out from under their feet.
SANDER- Charge at them and attempt to abrade any exposed skin.
SAUCER- Strike face and neck. Holding edgewise.
SAW- Slash at the face, neck, and hands.
SCISSORS- Jab at the eyes, neck, and temple.
SCREWDRIVER- Hold handle to stab at a vital areas or hold shaft for clubbing.
SCREWEYE- If it's large enough to clench, jab at their head, temple, eyes, ears, neck, and hands.
SHIT- Can be smeared on stabbing or cutting weapons to increase potency. They could be distracted if you could take a shit in a plastic bag and throw it in their face.
SHOES- Throw or use as a club, especially if they are high heel. Strike in it head, face, and neck with the high heel.
SHOVEL- Use blade to thrust and chop then deliver a blow with the flat side.
SIDEWALK- Throw them on the concrete and then smash their head repeatedly in it.
SILVER DOLLARS- Put them in a bag with a rope and swing it like a blackjack.
SKATEBOARD- Strike at his temple, nose, throat, hands, collarbone, and shins.
SKI POLES- Use as a lance or strike at head, arms, and chest with side and downward blows.

SMOKING PIPE- Holding like a gun, jab it in the eyes or grasp the stem and hammer on sensitive areas.
SOFA CUSHION-Use it as a shield against blunt weapon and knife attacks.
SOLDERING IRON-Clench it in your hand and drive it into the face, neck, solar plexus, and hands.
SPEAKERS- Pick up and strike at his head, chest, or use as a shield.
SPOON- Use it to gouge eyes or sharpen it into a knife.
STEAK KNIFE- Use it to slash at wrists and neck, stab at chest, or hammer blows into the shoulder and head.
STAIRWAY- If going up the stairs pretend to trip, kick him HARD in the groin backwards, and leap on him feet first. If going down, suddenly drop down on your heels and jerk his feet out from under him high.
STAPLER- The big office kinds closed can be used as brass knuckles and open as a small club to the head, face, or jaw. Construction type staple guns may be used in the same fashion.
SURFBOARD- Charge at them then swing it at their head, chest, and eyes.
TAPE MEASURE- Clench it and hammer at their head, nose, jaw, and ears.
TEETH- Attack at fingers, ears, nose, lips, throat, and sinus.
TELEPHONE- Detach it from the plug and swing it like a bola.
TENNIS RACKET- Give a chopping blow with the edge or jab handle into the abdomen or throat.
TOILET BRUSH- Brush end into eyes and use end of handle to hammer blows to the jaw.
TOOLBOX- Pick up and slam it at their head or swing it into their chest.
UMBRELLA- Jab at the throat, face, and solar plexus.
VASE- Throw it at them or club them in the head.
WALL- Grab his head and ram it into the wall.
WASP KILLER- Use as any other insecticide. However, wasp killer has a greater range and pin point accuracy.
WATCH- Slip over your knuckles and punch away.
WATER PISTOL- Fill it with noxious substances like ammonia, drain cleaner, strong acid, or corrosive chemicals. A super soaker type is great for this.
WHISKEY (or any other liquor)- Pour it on a roll of paper and ignite or take a swing and spit it in their eyes.

WIG– Can be set on fire and thrown at a attacker or can be used as a shield against knives.
WINDOW SHADE ROLLER- Use it as a club or a lance.
WRENCH- The bigger it is, the better. Strike at the head, ribs, neck, groin, and kneecaps.
YELLOW PAGES- The bigger the better, say like a Manhattan, NY or Chicago size makes a great shield against knife attacks.
YO-YO- Throw at their head, swing or hammer at vital areas with it.

Home Security

The three things intruders hate are places that are hard to get into, bright lights, and things that make noise. This is best done by having reinforced doors and windows, good outdoor lighting, and an alarm system and/ or a dog. However, everyone has different needs and budgets.

First, install deadbolt locks with a minimum one inch throw, door with a minimum of two inches of solid wood or wood covered with 16 gauge sheet metal, and a door frame of two inch wide wood or metal. Avoid hollow core doors and glass panel doors. Make sure the hinge pins are accessible only from the inside. Install security lights (spotlights with motion detectors are good) on the outside of the doors and porch. Place latches on all windows. If necessary install grillwork on all windows especially sliding glass doors or at least put in a dropstick. Consider installing polycarbonate windows that are shatterproof. Consider planting thorny plants around the residence like Bougainvillea, Upright Juniper, Mexican Palo Verde, Roses, Spanish Bayonet, Firethorn, and Dwarf Pomegranate. Put a security sign in front of your home- 'Home Protected by XXXX Alarm Co.', 'Property Under Video Surveillance', or my personal favorite 'Trespassers Will Be Shot. Survivors Will be Shot Again'. If you can afford it, consider a six-foot tall chainlink fence with barbed wire or razorwire on top.

If you have the space and time, getting a dog if a well worth asset for home security. It doesn't even to be overly aggressive because dogs do one thing that intruders hate- make noise. It could be a Labrador Retriever, Chow Chow, Terrier, or just a plain mutt if this is fine for you. However, if you want one that can be protective and not just bark- popular breeds include Dobermans, Bullmastiffs, Rottweilers, German Shepherds, Belgian Sheepdogs, Boviers, Akitas, American Bulldogs, Great Danes, and Rhodesian Ridgebacks. Go to your local animal shelter or breeder if you wish to get a puppy to train for protection. As an alternative some rural residents have been known for keeping certain birds such as geese which are aggressive and highly territorial or guinea fowl which are easily startled.

Alarm systems can be low tech or very high tech. What type you depends on what kind of neighborhood you live in and how much loot you have to rip-off. If you don't have much a good hiding place may be all you need. Low tech alarms can be as simple as putting breakable stuff on the windowsill, spike boards (wooden boards with long nails driven through them) below the windows on the floor, setting nails and broken glass in cement, tin cans on a string, or rigging one of those perimeter alarms to the door that fires 12 gauge blank shells. However, if you own many expensive goods you may need an ADT system with dispatch service and motion detecting video cameras. Most high tech alarm systems consist of entry sensors for doors and windows, infrared motion detectors for the inside, a base unit, and a very loud horn. Some have panic buttons and smoke detectors that automatically trigger an alarm. Good brands of electronic alarm systems include schlage, Universal Security, Tandy, and Black and Decker. Most can be self-installed saving you the cost of installation.

Last but not least, practice good security procedure. This sounds like common sense but you be surprised how many people don't do it. First of all besides keeping doors locked, identify all strangers before opening the door. If they claim to be from law enforcement or a utility- verify their ID first. Never give house keys to service workers. Some will copy them and burglarize you later. Always keep house keys separate from other keys and never put an address on them in case you lose them. Trim shrubbery and trees that can provider cover for intruders. When you leave home- leave the radio and lights on so intruders think the place is occupied. Put curtains on all the windows and close them at night. Hide or lockup all valuables (jewelry, optics, tools, electronics, and firearms) and take an inventory of them (write down the model, serial number, engrave them with a driver's license number- never social security number, and photograph). When you go on vacation- leave the radio on, cover the windows, and don't let mail pile in front of the house. Most burglars target unoccupied homes. Anyone who intrudes an occupied house is a dangerous threat! You should act accordingly. If possible, try to have a safe room as a retreat stocked with water, first aid kit, flashlights, pre-paid cell phone, weapons, and a bucket (you may in there for a while). It doesn't have to like the one in that movie Panic Room just a designated room where you can make your stand (like a bedroom). Install in this room solid core doors with deadbolt locks, heavy duty hinges, and window grills. For extra security, consider a crossbolt drop-in 2x4 barricade across the door as well.

Use of Booby-Traps

Booby-traps can be very useful against determined intruders as they have two uses one to remotely cause casualties and to induce fear in the intruder. They are best employed in footpaths behind doors, under the steps, and the base of walls or fences.

WARNING- The usage of booby-traps is **very** illegal and **very** dangerous. If an intruder is serious injured or killed and the police find out you **will** be charged with a felony and likely go to jail. You may also be open to civil liability by the injured party or their family. Use them at your own risk!!

(a) Spike boards- Drive long nails preferably rusty through square foot wooden blocks. The nails should be spaced 2-3". They are most effective in tall vegetation and darkened passages.

(b) Punji Stakes- Cut and sharpen copper or aluminum tubing, electrical conduit, TV antennas into stakes which are driven into the ground or set in concrete at a 30 degree or 40 degree angle around tall vegetation, stream beds, or ground pits.

(c) Fishhook Entanglement- String lines of fishhooks at face and chest level in narrow paths or thick foliage.

(d) Deadfalls- A heavy weight such as bricks, free weights, sack of rocks or broken glass, concrete, balls with spikes, or glass jars containing acid is suspended over a path where an intruder will trip a wire which is rigged to the trap.

(e) Light bulb Bomb- Turn off the light switch and remove the bulb from its socket. Drill a small hole in the upper neck of the bulb. Fill the bulb with gunpowder and plug the hole with electrical tape. **Warning! Make sure the light switch is off!!** Screw the bulb back in the socket. When an intruder flips on the light switch the bulb will explode.

(f) Hotfoots- A 12 gauge shell is placed in a metal sleeve. Attached to a piece of wood with a nail in it in a way that the shell extends slightly above the sleeve. It is pressure activated and can be placed in doorways or scattered in yards.

Use of Flash and Smoke Bombs

Discussing something like flash or smoke bombs may seem out of place in self-defense and more suited toward cheesy ninja movies or superhero comic books. However, SWAT teams and the military do use such pyrotechnics during their operations and so should not be dismissed out of hand. Flash bombs create an unexpected flash of light which can temporarily shock and blind aggressors. They are most effective in semi-dark or dark environments. Smoke bombs when ignited produce large amounts of smoke which can conceal a getaway route, create a diversion, or provide cover.

Flash bombs can be made yourself. However, it requires mixing chemicals which can be dangerous if mishandled. So remember some safety rules. No smoking (this should be obvious). Always mix chemicals with non-metal utensils. Always mix chemicals in small amounts not one big batch (you're mixing combustibles not baking a cake). First you will need flash paper and flash powder. Flash paper is treated paper that when ignited produces a bright flash. Commercial flash paper can be purchased at magician supply stores. You can make your own but it's a dangerous procedure so just buy it to be safe. Flash powder you'll have to make yourself but it is not difficult. Simply combine one part potassium nitrate (saltpeter) with one part powdered magnesium both of each can be purchased from chemical warehouses whom addresses I will list later. Now to make the flashbomb, envelop the flash powder in one sheet of flash paper and crumble it up. To ignite the flash bomb- light the paper with a lighter, match, or cigarette and throw.

Smoke bombs can come in the form of military smoke grenades, smoke distress signals, or the pyrotechnic kind. All can be purchased commercially. You can make your own too if you wish. As with the flash bombs, keep the same safety rules in mind. To make a flash/ smoke bomb combine one part gunpowder (such as Pyrodex) and one part powdered magnesium. Then envelop the powder with flash paper and ignite the same way as the flash bomb.

Since you are unlikely to find these chemicals in your local mall I listed some chemical warehouses which sell them. Note some of these places won't sell to individuals, in that case prepare a letter with a false business letterhead and under your signature add the title 'purchasing agent'.

Skylighter Inc., P.O. Box 480, Round Hill, VA 20142, (540) 338-0968, www.skylighter.com
Elemental Scientific LLC, P.O. Box 571, Appleton WI 54912, (920) 882-1277, www.elementalscientific.net
Firefox Enterprises Inc., P.O. 5366, Pocatello, ID 83202, (280) 237-1976, www.firefox-fx.com

PRIVACY

A little over a century ago a person could have had a reasonable amount of privacy. This is no longer the case as private sector and government institutions seek to further their amassing of data on their subjects to increase their control of them. The intention of these institutions wanting to do this is nothing new. However, with the technology available to them today is it easier than ever. To exacerbate this situation there's a cottage industry of growing information brokers who are willing to sell data on <u>you</u> to anyone for a profit. Even private individuals are getting in on the act- neighbors snooping on other neighbors, spouses snooping on each other, teachers, students, bosses, workers, even children trying to get the dirt on everyone else. In addition, databanks are increasingly sharing data with each other. If A shares data with C whom shares with B then A and even D (whom you don't know about yet until you try to apply for credit, insurance, or a loan) then they all have the same data, which many times aren't even accurate!

The Art of Invisibility

The best way to maintain invisibility from data collecting institutions is to 'fly under their radar' and maintain a low profile lifestyle. Flying under radar means basically leaving the least amount of a paper trail as possible. The four best ways to fly under radar is to- 1) Pay in cash, money order, or traveler's check only. Do NOT use credit cards. 2) Close all bank accounts in your name. 3) Have no bills in your name. 4) Keep your real name out of public records as much as possible (auto registration, any licensing (driver, marriage, and professional), property ownership, voter registration, and corporate filings). Different institutions track you in different ways. The IRS uses 1040 tax returns and W-2's, which are filed annually. They also are reported to about any transaction over $3,000 by banks (the government's snitch). The Social Security Administration (SSA) uses the National Directory of New Hires and employer payrolls which are filed quarterly. The police track by driver license whenever they are renewed and court records. Credit bureaus and collection agencies track you by credit card purchases and applications, loans, insurance policies, mortgages, voter registrations, bank accounts, and driver records. Even some supremarkets are tracking customer's purchases through "loyalty cards", avoid these or if you must use them use an alternate name (more on this later). In fact the private databases are frequently far more effective than the government ones!

Maintaining a low profile lifestyle means trying to not attract too much attention around your home, job, and lifestyle. Try not to look too rich or too poor. Vary your routine, avoid being predictable- use different routes, use different shops and restaurants. Dress modestly and drive a car that's not too flashy and fancy. Sanitize the car of anything advertising your work or private lifestyle. Buy your car used if possible. If you must buy a new car make sure it doesn't have OnStar or an EDR (Event Data Recorder) installed as these can track vehicles. If you are unsure about if the car has EDR or not check the owner's manual section about air bags. Do not use automatic toll lanes like the EZ Pass in New York. Keep you conservation with people you don't know well neutral, nothing controversial like religion, politics, or sexual practices. Do not volunteer information unless necessary. A store clerk doesn't need to your birthplace and occupation, leave it blank or if they bitch about it practice disinformation (fill in bullshit). Try using different versions of your name for example; John James Smith can be J. James Smith, J.J. Smith, or James Smith (see very easy, very legal). Avoid talking to the press. They frequently edit interviews to take what you said out of context or even distort it so much it seems like something different than you intended. Establish different levels of privacy- one for your spouse and children, a second for close family and friends, a third for acquaintances (other relatives, employers, co-workers, business relationships), and finally one for the public (everyone else). If you're into some 'funny business', be discrete about it not a loudmouth. Do not wear monogrammed jewelry or have custom vanity license plates. When anyone enters your home to do repairs, maintenance, delivery, or installation work- watch and stick with them! Make sure anything 'suspicious' (like your ninja sword collection, stack of Solider of Fortune magazines, books on satanic rituals, gay nazis and farm animals gone wild videos, empty liquor bottles, and bongs) are out of sight, preferably locked up. Many of these people will snitch you out especially for cash. One of the investigator's best tricks in his bag is to wave green pieces of paper with President Jackson on it in front of low wage clerks for information. Take care in what you say in the presence of heavy drug users, cabdrivers, ex-cops, ex-felons, bartenders, waitresses, relatives, and employers. They are common sources of information for investigators and cops. Beware of neighbors, co-workers, or landlords who are 'too friendly' or too eager to know your business if you just moved in or just got hired. Tell them only what you want them to know. Use the mushroom theory (keep them in the dark and feed them bullshit)!

Your Alternate Name and Address

The first line of your defense in maintaining privacy is to do not have your real name connected with your home address. Your home address should NEVER be given to any government or business entity you have contact with in your real name. Use an alternate address to get your mail in your real name. This can be a place of business, close friend or relative, church, homeless shelter or drop in center (my personal favorite), general delivery at the post office, or a squat. You can also consider using general delivery at an out-of-town post office. Another clever trick could be to get a decoy rural address by digging a hole and putting in a post with a mailbox at the intersection of a long row of rural mailboxes. You can even combine this with another alternate address! Avoid using post office boxes or commercial mailboxes such as Postnet or Mailboxes. These are not secure! Government agencies keep a database of commercial mailbox companies. Use only if the address on your ID isn't your true address. In addition, if the alternate address is a close relative or friend give them specific instructions not to give your address and telephone number (if they have it) to ANYONE without your consent. Investigators, cops, and snoops will use a variety of pretexts and social engineering to trick them into revealing personal information.

This alternate address you should use for the IRS, DMV, real estate, loans, pet license, hunting and fishing licenses, concealed carry weapon permits, library card, voter registration, insurance policies, utility companies, cable TV, internet service, property taxes, licensing and certification boards, building permits, doctors, dentists, attorneys, accountants, memberships, social security, video rentals, titles, purchases, public assistance, medicare, moving companies, passports, colleges, and employers. Employers are especially important because I-5 forms go to immigration and W-4 forms go to the IRS. Also employees working at agencies with access to your applications can be bribed by private investigators and crooks to find you. Likewise ID tags for luggage, keys, etc. should have the alternate address only. If you wish to be truly discrete consider using two, three, even five alternate addresses! If you have your real name connected with your home address now, change it and get an alternate address now! Although moving is the only certain way of breaking the connection, as a stop-gap clean up the trail by calling businesses that have your address already and give them the 'new' address (like an abandoned house, biker bar, or gas station). When you get it do NOT notify the post office of your new address. They are databases in existence that find people's new addresses based on postal mail forwarding cards and new utility hookup orders. It might seem like a lot of work but the peace of mind you get will be worth it. You could even consider getting a driver's license out of state. Get a new license from your original state that is used to get another license in a different state. When filing out the application change one digit in your date of birth and one letter in your name, then use an alternate address. Consider establishing a dual-state residency, you could live in Florida but have a license in New York then open a post office box in Florida with the New York address. Register the car out of state too (more on this later). Also use false mother maiden names. Finally, do not file change of address cards as their databases are sold to credit bureaus and skip tracers.

Your alternate name (aka- pseudonym, assumed name, stage name, penname, or nom de guerre) is your cover name for services not requiring ID. The more common this name is the better; check your local white pages for this. <u>ALL</u> mail going to your real address should be in your alternate name only. This includes email, pager or voicemail service, utilities and video stores on cash deposit, signatories on bank accounts, approved user of credit cards, and titles. If you join a sports or hobby association or organization use an alternate name. If you must politically campaign use an alternate name. If you are getting a package from FedEx, UPS, DHL, or Airborne Express use an alternate name <u>only</u> as they keep national databases on names and addresses. If you are participating in a survey or whatever give them an alternate name. If you get your newspaper delivered to your home use an alternate name. If you're even going to get some Chinese food, a pizza, or some beer delivered use a fucking alternate name! Domino's and Pizza Hut keep databases too!! Also when signing your name- real or alternative, the more illegible it is the better (sign it like a doctor)! One last thing, if you use a moving company- no real name for them either. They have been known to sell lists of new addresses to marketers.

Mail, Trash, and Utilities

When mailing a letter do not place your name on the return address, use only an address and zip code. If the post office has the zip code only they can still find the city and state. If you receive mail of a political, religious, sexual, or other controversial nature definitely use an alternate name. If you're writing to request mail of a questionable nature, use a return address far away from your true mailing address and write it on the back as the USPS photocopies every front of envelopes (yes they do!). Opt-out of mailing lists in your real name. Do not buy postage online or use postage meters, as they leave a paper trail. Don't file census forms either as they collect much demographic data which could provide some information on your lifestyle to a clever investigator. Magazine subscriptions should be in an alternate name. To circumvent unwanted mail, write 'addressee unknown- return to sender', 'addressee moved', or 'deceased' on the envelope and drop it in an out of town mailbox. Freon, which is widely available, can be used to secretly read your mail. So if you're mailing anything sensitive wrap the contents with aluminum foil, insert it in an envelope, and then put that in a larger envelope. Your mailbox should have a lock on it to prevent thieves from stealing mail looking for checks, cash, or information to steal identities. Never leave outgoing mail in an unprotected box. Use a pickup station, your work, USPS mailbox, or give it to the mailman only.

Trash has represented a godsend to privacy invaders for years. It used to be only the destitute, hackers, and investigators in on the secret. Not anymore, everyone dumpster dives these days. There are even books and web pages up about it! I've been doing myself for over ten years and I found some very interesting things (like people's credit reports!). Therefore, if your trash has personal information and can be read it must be shredded, bleached, burned, or otherwise destroyed. This includes bank statements, telephone bills, utility bills, canceled checks, credit card statements, paycheck and money order stubs, prescription bottles, personal letters, matchbooks with phone numbers, and health insurance statements. If you use a shredder it should be of the crosscutting type for maximum privacy. Documents can be bleached by soaking them in a bucket of water mixed with half-cup of bleach. Always take your credit card and atm receipts with you then burn them and flush them down the toilet. Even innocuous things like grocery receipts, pharmacy slips, cut out classified ads, and old 'suspicious' magazines should be destroyed or at least put in a public trashcan. An observant person can determine your lifestyle from red flags like excessive booze, birth control, chronic illness, gay or alternative sexual lifestyle, interest in weapons, or other 'bizarre' practices. Finally, avoid leaving sensitive trash at places like Kinko's, Staples, or the post office as I've personally found resumes, faxes, and discarded mail in these.

If you wish to get anonymous utilities use cash deposit in a money order or a cashier's check and place a password on the account. Give them your alternate address only. NEVER use your real social security number, real name, or real date of birth. If you pay a deposit in advance they usually don't care about a social security number but if they hassle you about this, tell them you're from Canada or Australia (this usually works). Medical care involving mental problems or disease, alcohol and drug abuse, or abortion should be done under an alternate name and if possible paid in cash and done in another state.

Your Social Security Number

The social security number (SSN) almost single handedly represents one of the greatest threats to privacy. It was never intended for that purpose when it was created in the 1930's for a retirement fund. Since then more and more public and private agencies started using it for record keeping to the point that it today is a de facto serial number. The United States Armed Forces, IRS,

Passport Office, federal employers, and welfare departments use it as a serial number by law. Licensing records at the secretary of state office, DMV, court records, voter registrars, employees, banks, landlords, loan and insurance companies make use of it as well. Only recently because of the increase in identity theft has the public become aware of the implications of giving out those nine little digits out liberally.

The only time you are required to provide to provide your SSN is to government agencies (for a driver or other license or to get benefits), employers , banks, and getting credit. If possible when applying for a job do not provide your SSN unless you are actually hired for the job. In the space that says SSN write 'provided upon employment' instead. If anyone else asks for your SSN, use generic SSN's or just one make up. Some generic SSN's are 022-28-1852, 042-10-3580, 062-36-0749, 078-05-1120 (this is the most popular one!), 095-07-3645, 128-03-6045, 135-01-6629, 141-18-5941, 155-18-7999, 165-15-7999, 165-20-7999, 165-22-7999, 165-24-7999, 189-02-2294, 212-09-7694, 219-09-9999, 306-30-2348, 308-12-5070, 468-28-2779 and 549-24-1889. Some people think this is illegal. It is NOT unless you are trying to deceive a government agency (such as the police, IRS, welfare, DMV, passport office), commit fraud, or trying to get a specific benefit (like credit or a loan). Everyone else (hospitals, colleges, landlords, utilities, video rental, retail stores, insurance companies) gets a generic SSN. Do not give your SSN to the DMV unless required. If they require it avoid having it printed on the license.

There is no law that states you must give your SSN for utilities, medical care, casual labor, police reports, and even firearm applications. If you still feel guilty about using a generic number then tweak your number a bit or what I call form dyslexia. For example, a1 can become a 7 (this is why people used to put slashes in 7's) and a 4 a 9. If they 'discover' your 'mistake', tell them it must have been a data entry error or some other bullshit.

Like I said before checks and credit cards should avoided for maximum privacy however if you must use checks or credit cards follow these rules. If you pay by check, provide your ID only. Do NOT put your SSN or credit card number on the check. If you pay by credit card, provide no ID beyond your signature. Do NOT provide your address or SSN. Do not carry your social security card, credit cards, or checks in your wallet unless you need it in case of loss or theft. You should photocopy all cards in your wallet as well. The best ID for privacy is a passport because your SSN is not printed on them. It is a good idea not to provide your true date of birth unless required by law either. Give them your legal age or make it up, especially for medical records. Finally, needless to say NEVER give out your SSN over the telephone.

Using Telephones

First of all let's state that there's no such thing as complete phone privacy, only more privacy or less privacy. When using the phone assume someone is listening and know a record **will** somewhere be made of all calls (be it voice, fax, pager, data, etc.). Your telephone should only be in your alternate name, a liaison's name, or if impossible ask them to list the phone in an alternate name but keep your middle name and last name on their files. Tell them you want to opt out of CPNI (Customer Proprietary Network Information), their information sharing racket. This includes records of the services you use, type of calls you make, and a log of the numbers you called. Unlisted numbers are false security, because when you call an 800, 888, or 900 number they use Automatic Number Identification (ANI) which reveals your phone number even if it's unlisted. When calling 911 an ANI system is used as well. Post the local number to the police and fire department instead (you may even get quicker service this way). Use a pay phone or a friend's phone for these numbers. Never give out personal information to solicitors. If telemarketers start calling sign up with the National Do Not Call Registry at 1-888-382-1222 or www.donotcall.gov online. While you're at it, opt out for prescreened credit offers too at 1-888-5OPTOUT and opt-out other databases (you can get nice big list for this at http://www.privacyrights.org/ar/infobrokers-optout.htm). Answer the phone with a 'hello' only. Do not give out names until the caller is identified and cleared. If you are making calls you rather noone know about clearing the redial and caller ID would be a good idea too. You'd be surprised how many cheating spouses have been busted this way!

If you wish keep someone from using caller ID against you they're several methods for doing this. One is to dial *67 before making the call. Two problems with this is the caller ID will display 'private' alerting the person and this does NOT work with 800, 866, 877, 888, 900, 976 numbers and 911. Another is to call from a pay phone in an airport, mall, hotel, or college. But the caller ID may display 'pay phone' plus you can be traced back to the location. Another way is to use a prepaid card but some cards will pass caller ID info to the recipient. Best to test the card first on a phone with caller ID, if it displays 'out of area' then it's safe. Other ways involve calling from an office phone attached to a PBX (public branch exchange) or having the operator dial the number for you. The best method would be to use caller ID spoofing services which are widely available on the internet.

There's a new company called Reconex (www.reconex.com) which offers prepaid landline service. No identification, social security number, or credit is needed. There are no deposits and you get unlimited local service plus a certain amount of long distance minutes (usually 60). They can be contacted at 1-800-275-8223 but they aren't available in every state and are sort of expensive ($50 to $80 per month depending upon the state).

If you get a cordless phone use a spread-spectrum digital 900 MHz or 2.4 GHz model only. Avoid the old style analog cordless phones, as they are very unsecure. A couple of years ago a roommate and I were listening to a scanner and picked up a lady making death threats (like arranging a gas explosion) over a cordless phone!! We even used it as a sample in an industrial music project. The digital models are difficult to eavesdrop on because the signal sounds like noise. Unless a three-letter government agency (think FBI, CIA, or NSA) is after you, you're pretty safe.

You shouldn't identify yourself on an answering machine either. Just leave the last four digits of your number and a crazy recording. Get obnoxious if you wish, after all it is your answering machine. However, eavesdroppers can listen to messages by hacking the remote control feature. The access codes on these are very weak using only 3 digits. All one has to do is start dialing 123,

111, 222, birthdays, etc. or just use the default code 000 which most people don't bother changing. A law enforcement supplier 'Shomer-tec' even sells an automatic hacker called the 'Answering Machine Intruder.' Change the default code and change it often. Do not call it from cordless or cell phone because someone with a scanner can listen to the touch-tones and copy them.

Pagers (one-way ONLY not two-way) using Pagenet and Skytel are a very secure way to receive incoming calls because you can get one without ID, have a voice mailbox so you can screen your calls, and can't be tracked. On your PIN for the voice mailbox be sure to change the default, change it often, and do not call it from a cordless or cell phone. Use your real phone number for only close friends and family. Everyone else gets the voicemail number. Faxing from a public place is the best for privacy. If you must fax from your home use caller ID blocking, do not fax to any 800 numbers, and remove or falsify header information the fax automatically sends.

Do not use personal phone credit cards as your calls can be traced. Use prepaid phone cards brought with cash, as they can be secure. Some of them actually automatically block caller ID and ANI, plus long distance numbers won't show on the telephone bill. To be ultraprivate, write down the number, alter the last two digits with two easy to remember digits, and destroy the card. Avoid using payphones in big airports, bus terminals, police stations, courts, government buildings, and places known for drug activity or prostitution as they may be tapped.

I did not like cellular phones at first but they are so popular with the right precautions can be used with fair privacy. First of all do not get a cellphone in your own name! Use a liaison (more on this later) or use a pre-paid cellphone. They are very good prepaid providers out there such as Tracfone, Net10, Pageplus, Virgin, and T-mobile. Always pay cash and buy the maximum minutes you can afford. Upon activation give no identifying information whatsoever. Place a password on the phone to protect the data on it in case it's stolen. For maximum privacy (like if you're a dope dealer or just like to wear tin foil hats); you can get several phones- one for your 'inner circle', another for your alternate name, one more for really sensitive conversations. Then give away or sell the phone when the number expires since names may get attached to the phone. In addition, incoming calls could go to a voice mail box number and outgoing calls can go through a prepaid phone card first. A good free service for this is Grand Central (www.grandcentral.com), they give you a phone number which you can give out and any incoming calls to that number automatically get forwarded to one or more hidden phone numbers of your choice. If you're really paranoid, do not turn it on except to call out (cells can be tracked when on) or make calls inside as GPS sometimes has difficulty getting a fix inside buildings. Also, turn off location based services (if any) with the cellphone's menu function. If 911 is dialed on any cellphone it can be isolated within 300 feet by the E911 system and certain cell tracking sites such as Vlocate and Followus exist. When speaking on a cell be vague, use only first names, and do not use organization names. Be sure to remind the other party you are on a cell phone. If sensitive details must be discussed, set up a call-in number. Do NOT use text messaging for sensitive matters. All messages (including content) are logged by the phone service company!! If you must text message someone else use this website www.AnonTxt.com for anonymous texting. Avoid using Bluetooth as it can be hacked by a technique known as bluesnarfing. If you do use it protect yourself by keeping the firmware updated, use long pin's, do not pair devices in public, and do not leave Bluetooth on after using and in a discoverable mode. By the way, Texas just passed a law requiring ID for prepaid cell purchase and limits you to only five per purchase.

If you replace your cell it is important that you wipe the cell phone memory and remove the SIM card. The SIM card may only have the contact list but the internal memory may be storing call logs, photos, memos, text messages, and call timers. If the cell has data synchronization go to www.recellular.com and use 'Cell Phone Data Eraser'. Choose the brand and model of your phone and follow the instructions.

Now the precautions I just mentioned may should a little too 'cloak and dagger' but cell phones can be easily intercepted. Secondary 'harmonic' signals from cells can be periodically picked up from 'old style' analog TV sets (the ones that used to go to channel 83) and illegal scanners. Even though the federal government banned the manufacture of scanners capable of receiving cell phone signals, pre-ban scanners still exist. Cell capable scanners can be brought in Canada and Mexico. Some tech-savvy people alter scanners to make them cell capable or use computer-aided scanners. They are commercial cell monitoring systems coasting about $2,000-$3,000 for law enforcement agencies on the market. Cells can also be tracked through radio triangulation. There is even a cell tracing set available to (you guessed it) law enforcement agencies for about $35,000, which can track you even if you aren't talking as long as the cell is on. Finally, the NSA (National Security Agency) monitors every overseas phone call and microwave phone transmission (many of which are located in the United States).

Want to try a fun experiment? You need a cell capable scanner and a frequency counter. The Optoelectronics Scout for about $350 is a good model. Follow someone walking down the street talking on a cell phone. Take the frequency counter and get the frequency when it latches on the cell phone signal. Then punch that frequency in a pre-ban scanner and bingo you can listen in!

If you're really paranoid I've heard of a secure cell phone which uses a random ESN (electronic serial number) and phone number every time it's used meaning it calls under and bills a different number on every call! They are very expensive and obviously very illegal, but they do exist and no, I don't know where you can find one.

Using Computers

First rule is there is no such thing as a completely secure computer. If you buy a new computer, do not fill in your real name, address, phone number, or other personal information for registration, software, internet service provider, etc. Put in false information like a name 'Atilia D. Hun, an address in Georgia (not the U.S. state but the country bordering Russia), and a phone number in Brazil. If you buy a used computer and someone's name is on it, leave it on. Don't place your name on it. Then immediately place a BIOS password on the computer in addition to one for the account on the operating system. If the new computer is replacing the old computer, take out the old hard drive, erase it, torch it, smash it to smithereens with a hammer, and dispose the pieces in different places. All obsolete disks with sensitive data should be overwritten, formatted, demagnetized, and burned not just tossed in the trash. CD-ROM's can be microwaved for 15 seconds prior to destruction. Thumb drives should be overwritten and destroyed as well. I couldn't begin to tell you the amount of unerased disks I've found in the trash.

When you delete a file, it is NOT gone. It just frees up the space on that part of the disk to be overwritten. Certain utility programs such as Undelete (www.diskeeper.com), Active@undelete (www.active-undelete.com), Disk Investigator (www.theabsolute.net/sware/dskinv.html) , or Easy Recovery Pro (www.ontrackdatarecovery.com) can read it! Sensitive data should be kept on removable drives, thumb drives, memory cards, or CD-ROM's (in music CD cases) only and put in a safe place. If you must have your computer repaired remove ALL sensitive data from the hard drive. Technicians have been approached by cops to report any suspected criminal activity on a computer. They are some programs that completely overwrite the data on the drive. Three good sources which offer free programs are Eraser (www.heidi.ie/eraser) and Ultrawipe (www.snapfiles.com). Some other good ones are BCwipe (www.jetico.com), Evidence Eliminator (www.evidence-eliminator.com), and Cyberscrub (www.cyberscrub.com). After overwriting the data, the drive should defragmented, and overwritten again with a different program if possible. Never should sensitive data be kept on a fixed hard drive (especially on laptops!). Any sensitive data should be further encrypted with a good encryption program such as Truecrypt (www.truecrypt.org), BC Archive (www.jetico.com), Finecrypt (www.finecrypt.net), Kruptos 2(www.kruptos2.co.uk) or Cryptainer PE (www.cypherix.co.uk). Never use the DES algorithm for encryption, as it has been broken. Use only 3-DES, RC6, Blowfish, Twofish, or AES algorithms for encryption. Over time computers regularly used accumulate track files which should be wiped periodically. These include the paging (swap) file which should wiped when the computer is shutdown (Eraser can do this) and any free space or clusters on the hard drive which should be wiped at least weekly.

If you use a computer at work 1) never send an email you wouldn't your boss to see, 2) be careful what you type- **very** careful. Many companies use software on their systems that can record keystrokes, log website visits, and monitor program use. This is all perfectly legal and since it is their computer there isn't much you can do about it.

Try to use free web-based e-mail services whenever possible. Avoid using your ISP's e-mail (it's just too easy to home in on you). Never use information that will revel your true identity or address. Always use an alternate name, preferably gender-neutral or just using initials (online harassers mostly seek out females). Some good web-based e-mails include Gmx.com, Yahoo.com, Aim.com, Inbox.com, and Fastmail.com. Try to diversify your e-mail addresses have one for family and friends, another for business, and another one for everyone else. If you are forwarding emails to a lot of people use the BCC (blind carbon copy) field. Sending e-mail is like sending a postcard. Anyone with the technical know-how, time, and money can read it. Assume that anything in an e-mail will be read by others. This goes double for IM (Instant Messaging), best to avoid altogether.

All passwords created should be unpredictable, have at least eight characters, have digits and letters, and have uppercase and lowercase letters. Do not create dumb passwords using nicknames, people's names, middle names, addresses, phone numbers, social security numbers, driver's license numbers, date of birth's, and simple patterns (i.e.- asdfgh). Avoid words in the dictionary and proper nouns as well in any language. A good method is to use the first letters of a short sentence you'll remember or substitute symbols for vowels (like making an A a @). Hackers use dictionary word lists in password cracking programs. Passwords should never be written near the computer, put in wallets, or stored in computer files. Use a password manager like Keepass (www.keepass.info) or the one built-in the Firefox browser which encrypts all your passwords in a single file, some even generate random ones, and you only need a single master password to access it. Keep this file on a thumb drive or other removable media so it's not stored on your main computer. Changing them periodically is a good idea as well, monthly to yearly depending on sensitivity. Needless to say, never share passwords with anyone else.

If you are sending anything by an e-mail program you don't want read use an encryption programs like Pretty Good Privacy (PGP), GPG, or Enigmail for Thunderbird. Use caution though while the message cannot be read without the proper keys the senders and receivers can be identified. True anonymous email uses Mixmaster (like mixminion or 2remail) and Quicksilver software, however these can be difficult to configure and not for novices. Some secure low-cost e-mail services which offer virus protection and are spam free include Safe-mail and Ziplip. While others like Hushmail (www.hushmail.com), Cryptomail (www.cryptomail.org), Certifiedmail.org (www.certifiedmail.com), and MailVault (www.mailvault.com) offer free encrypted webmail, but both the sender and recipient must have accounts. Also consider looking into steganography programs that hide the text inside picture files like .gif and .jpg, mp3 music files, and video files like .avi. One good source for this is Steganos Security Suite from www.steganos.com. Other steganography programs can be found on www.stegoarchive.com and www.jjtc.com/Security/stegtools.htm. I'd strongly advise against sending anything sensitive over IM but if you do look into programs called IMsecure (www.zonelabs.com), Bitwise IM (www.bitwiseim.com), Hush Messenger (www.hushmail.com), and Simppro (www.secway.fr) which encrypts IM text but the sender and receiver must have the software.

When using your computer to surf the internet you need to use caution as well. The first thing you must have if you have nothing else is a good anti-virus software program that should be updated regularly and whenever a new virus alert is announced. Well-reputed anti-virus programs include Kaspersky Antivirus (www.kaspersky.com), Norton Antivirus (www.symantec.com), Bitdefender (www.BitDefender,com), and Nod32 (www.eset.com). Also look into AVG AntiVirus (www.grisoft.com), Avast (www.avast.com), and Avira AntiVir (www.free-av.com) all which happens to be free as well. If you wish to do a quick checkup for viruses try online scanners such as Nanoscan (www.nanoscan.com) and Trend Micro Housecall (housecall.trendmicro.com). Mailreaders , web browsers, and office software should be updated with patches affecting security as well. A site called www.secunia.com can help since it inspects your programs to see if they are out of date. Avoid Internet Explorer browsers and use Firefox or Opera instead. Use Mozilla's Thunderbird or Pegasus instead of Microsoft's Outlook for a mailreader. Switch from Microsoft Office to Openoffice too. Never boot the computer with an unknown disk in the floppy drive. Never download files sent by strangers or click on hyperlinks and attachments in emails from senders you don't know. Do not use the autocomplete feature on passwords. Use phishing filters on browsers. Disable file and print sharing on systems. Some have been linked with virus outbreaks. If you use chat rooms or Usenet never disclose personal information. If you do social networking have no identifying information whatsoever (name, address, email, phone #, date of birth, work, or education) on your profile and put ALL pictures under private. Make your profile photo an avatar. Employers and law enforcement are increasingly using these for checks. Avoid using automatic online bill paying. If you must use a credit card or enter personal info on a commerce site, make sure it's HTTPS secure (look for the closed padlock icon at the bottom of the sceen or https in the website address) and a Verisign certificate. When using public computers ask about their security policy and be aware that some people may have keyloggers unlawfully installed on the computer. You can find hardware keyloggers by checking for a small cylinder connected to the keyboard cable and the computer. Software keyloggers however are harder to detect and require a key logger detector program such as KL Detector (www.dewasoft.com) which may not be able to be installed on a public computer. Also avoid using copiers with network connections (like the ones in Kinko's) for personal information because it stores the copies digitally on their system. Use a personal copier or the ones in schools, libraries, or grocery stores instead.

Internet broadband connections using cable or DSL are vulnerable to attack because the connection is always open. Choose an Internet Provider with online virus and spam filters. Turn on the hardware firewall also known as NAT (network address translation) and SPI (stateful packet inspection) that's built into the router. Then protect the connection further with an installed firewall program also to counter hackers whom scan for unprotected connections to steal data or take over computers. Some good firewall programs include Zonealarm Pro (www.zonelabs.com), Outpost Pro (www.agnitum.com), and Kerio Personal (www.sunbelt-software.com). Decent free alternatives include Comodo Firewall Pro (www.personalfirewall.comodo.com), Online Armor Personal (www.tallemu.com), NetVeda Safety.Net (www.netvada.com), and Jetico Personal (www.jetico.com). Then to make should your firewall is configured correctly test it with free online resources at Shields Up! (www.grc.com) and PC Flank (www.pcflank.com). Digital track files such as cookies, temp files, history, old emails, and caches should be deleted after each internet session. Doing this manually can be cumbersome but some programs like Evidence Eliminator (www.evidence-eliminator.com), Window Washer (www.webroot.com), Privacy Suite (www.cyberscrub.com), and CrapCleaner (www.ccleaner). Some programs are available which destroys 'spyware' that infiltrates computers from the internet. Good free ones are AVG Anti-Spyware Free (www.grisoft.com), A-squared Free (www.emsisoft.com), Spycatcher Express (www.tenebril.com) and Windows Defender (www.microsoft.com). Other commercial anti-spyware software includes Spysweeper (www.webroot.com), Counterspy (www.sunbelt-software.com), Spyware Doctor (www.pctools.com). If you wish to keep your browsing anonymous look into pay private proxy servers like www.anonymizer.com, www.idzap.com, www.megaproxy.com; free open proxies such as www.the-cloak.com, www.cloakip.net, www.hidemyass.com (got to love that name), and www.anonymouse.org; or the free software OperaTor (http://archetwist.com/en/opera/operator) and Vidalia(http://vidalia-project.net) designed to access the web through TOR's network of encrypted proxies. These sites block access to your computer by using proxy servers so websites can't place cookies on it and identity your IP address (which can be used to trace you). Last but not least keep current on issues concerning web security. Some good sites for the information include CERT (www.cert.org), Gibson Research- Shields Up! (www.grc.net), Internet Computer Security Association (www.icsa.net), Microsoft Security Advisor (www.microsoft.com/security), and Zdnet's Security Page (www.zdnet.com/enterprise/secuirty). Finally, consider using browsers such as Mozilla Firefox or Opera instead of Microsoft Internet Explorer which have stronger security protocols.

Although this may be overkill for most people, if you wish to use some hardcore protection do this. First, install an intrusion prevention system which protects from non-signature anti-spyware and zero-day attacks. Good IPS software include Threatfire (www.threatfire.com), Prevx1(www.prevx.com), Safeconnect (www.sanasecurity.com), Blink Personal, and Winpatrol. Then, install a rootkit scanner- rootkits are like cloaking devices for malware. Good sources for these include Panda Anti-Rootkit (,http://www.pandasecurity.com/homeusers/downloads/docs/product/help/rkc/en/rkc_en.htm) , AVG Anti-rootkit (www.grisoft.com), Rootkit Revealer (www.sysinternals.com), Blacklight (www.f-secure.com/blacklight/), or Darkspy (www.softpedia.com). Finally, whenever you use your browser isolate it in a virtual environment to protect the main operating system from malware with a program like Sandboxie (www.sandboxie.com), Defensewall (www.softsphere.com), or Bufferzone (www.trustwave.com).

Many people have installed private wireless networks in their homes and businesses. These should be avoided and never used for sensitive information. Many hackers engage in a technique known as wardriving, in which they drive around the city with special antennas, a laptop, hacktools like Netstumbler or Airopeek and pick up network traffic. If you must install a private wireless network make sure to follow these steps. Change the default administrative password on the router. Check that software for drivers and WPA on the adapter are up to date. Enable the firewall, change the default SSID (system id) and disable its broadcasting. Filter the MAC addresses allowed on the on the hardware. Enable the highest level of WPA encryption (not WEP which is extremely weak) with decent keys. Use strong encryption for all applications used on the network (for example SSL, TLS/HTTPS). Encrypt all wireless traffic using a VPN (virtual private network). Disable DHCP and assign manually a static IP address to each computer and device in the network. Also, disable remote administration, enable computer and router firewalls at all times, and shut down the network after use. Call me a little too much twentieth century but I'll skip this whole process and just stick with cables and wires, it just doesn't seem worth the trouble.

If you have a laptop and are using a network in a public place like a café, fast food place, library, hotel, or an airport be REAL careful. They are also known as hotspots and can get you in some real hot water unless you take certain precautions. Most hotspots are considered public and do NOT use encryption meaning all real-time traffic sent will be in the clear! To prevent an unauthorized connection to your computer enable and keep updated all your firewall and antivirus software. Use a good administrative password; disable both the peer to peer mode and filesharing options. Try to limit your activity to general browsing. However, if you must use email, file transfer, use IM, or send sensitive information make sure the website, FTP, or email client is using SSL encryption for login and message exchange. Using a personal VPN between the laptop and router at the hotspot will protect against any eavesdropping and will increase your privacy greatly. This is actually your best protection. Some good sources for this are Hotspot Shield (www.anchorfree.com), iPig Wifi Hotspot Vpn (www.iopus.com), Hotspot Helper (www.jiwire.com), personalVPN (www.witopia.net), and Personal VPN (www.boingo.com). For extra protection against unsafe hotspots get Airdefense Protection Lite (www.airdefense.net). Turn off the network connection when not in use and disable the auto connect to open wi-fi access points.

One last thing, there is no such thing as a completely secure computer. The most secure computer in the world is a brand new one that is NEVER put online and buried in a concrete vault encased in a faraday cage 100 feet underground.

Privacy in Traveling

In general, the most private modes of travel are by ground on bus, car, or train. Air travel has always been the least anonymous and even more so after 9/11 in the United States. Post 9/11 Amtrak requires photo ID and even some bus lines require it. However, they are some 'tricks' one can use to maximize privacy. The first is to pay cash whenever possible with air travel being the exception. Trying to pay cash for a plane ticket actually arouses suspicion! Consider buying your plane ticket from a travel agency with a money order or cashier's check. Also, initial your first name and use only your last name on the plane ticket. For extra privacy, use your first name and 'misspell' your last name (i.e. Sam Riddle would become Sam Middle). If you're stopped by security tell them it was a 'clerical error'. Travel with small airlines and do not get your passport stamped. If you are going overseas, consider traveling to your destination indirectly. Go to Canada or Mexico first then fly to nearby country and take the train or bus to your destination. If possible, do not charge foreign tickets to credit cards. If you purchase a travel package do not use travel agencies as they keep records on where you flew, booked a hotel, rented a car, and even how far you drove.

When dealing with airport security- travel during high traffic periods (they will have less time to scrutinize you). In addition, minimize your carry on luggage, put all metal objects (keys, watch, pens, buckles) in checked luggage, and lock your checked luggage. Do not take provocative or controversial reading material aboard, keep it in checked luggage. Passengers have been harassed for this before.

At your destination, avoid renting cars and use taxis or public transportation instead. If you must rent a car go to local small firms, avoid the big companies. Do not use your home address, but an alternate one instead. Read the agreement to make sure the car isn't tracked by GPS (Global Positioning System) or has a EDR (Event Data Recorder) sort of a black box for cars installed. Avoid toll roads. If you must use them, pay cash only never by an automated toll collection system.

Do not use hotels, as they demand ID, especially the five star hotels. They are very insecure! Besides having many surveillance cameras sometimes the elevators and even the payphones are monitored! Use local motels and hostels paying cash only. Never charge calls to your room use a calling card. Avoid using their payphones as well as the line may be monitored. If possible stay with family, friends, or climate and law enforcement permitting a squat or camp out for the most privacy. Finally, do not volunteer information to strangers, try to blend in, and keep your big mouth shut!

Use of Liaisons

A liaison is a person who on your behalf- opens up a bank account, gets a cell phone, signs up for utilities, or signs a lease. You can use close friends or trusted relatives (ones you don't see too often if possible), someone who owes you a favor, or someone who has little or no assets such as homeless people, college students, or illegal aliens. Just pay the liaison a small fee or gratuity for providing this service for you. Caution though it is best to use liaisons investigators won't make quick connections to like parents, boy/girlfriends, or spouses. It will be the first place they will look.

Use of Banks

Opening an account at the bank represents a significant privacy concern. The banker is essentially the government's snitch. Any cash transaction over $5,000 is automatically reported to the IRS by a form 8300 filing. In addition, any wire transfer over $750 plus they identify the sender AND receiver. The best way to address this is to have no account at all but to use only cash, postal money orders, cashier's checks, traveler's checks, and direct deposit debit cards (aka- prepaid credit cards). Cash payroll checks at the employer's bank or a check cashier. Lesser known ways such as barter, gold/ silver coins, Mexican/ Canadian banks, and foreign credit cards may be used as well. Be careful though any cash transaction over $3,000 for postal money orders and over $750 for overseas wire transfers has to be reported by ALL financial service businesses (including check cashers and money wiring services). However, the not having a bank account option is not very viable for many people.

The next alternative for the not so paranoid is to open a new account in another state or even another country (like Canada or Mexico) where you can get a local address. Choose the smallest or credit union with no out-of-state branches. Visit the bank when it's busy like Friday or a payday. When you open the account opt on any information sharing they may do. Once, the new account is open close your old account to prevent any back trails. Never visit the bank again and do all your banking through ATM. Withdraw your money from the ATM first then make your purchases. Never make your purchases directly from the ATM card as the leaves a paper trail. Deposit money by mail with a money order ONLY. After the account has been open several months change the local address to your alternate address. Never tell them your true address or phone number. If you must use checks, never use their checks as this leaves a trail on the bank statement. Mail order your own from places like Checks in the Mail (1-800-292-8966) and Checks Unlimited (1-800-565-8332) noting on the reorder form or voided check to place only your first initial and last name (no street address) on the checks. If you have your own computer and the right hardware/ software you can even print your own checks.

The next level for more privacy is to use a liaison to open the account for you. Pick a bank in a state where you and the liaison don't live. Make out a bank cashier's check over the minimum deposit to the liaison and have them open the account. Mail order some checks but <u>not</u> from the bank without addresses printed on them and high check numbers starting at 8001 or higher so as to 'age' the account. When the checks come have the liaison sign every one until finished. You keep all the checks and use them as you wish. In addition, banks report account activity to the IRS in January annually. So keep the balance low and use a non-interest bearing account. If your really paranoid, move your account in January or February to another bank if you don't want the account traced. On an endnote, beware of depositing unknown checks into your own account but take it to the bank it was drawn instead. This is an old investigator's trick to find out where one does their banking

Another thing that may be useful to the privacy seeker is this prepaid debit card that has come to my attention. It's a called a Simon Gift Card it can be purchased in cash with no questions asked at any of the several hundred Simon Malls across the country. Check out their web site (www.simon.com/findamall/) if you don't know where a store is located. They are purchased once for $6 then can be loaded from a value of $20-$500 and used anywhere that a Visa card is accepted. Another one is the All Access Gift Card (www.allaccessgift.com), which can be purchased for $5 and loaded with an amount from $25 to $250. The beauty with these cards is that they can be used to buy services and merchandise online or transfer cash safely to another person or account albeit anonymously. Always pay cash for them and never personalize them. If you intend to make purchases online, mail, or phone you'll have to 'register' it with your name, address, phone #, and email. Just give them a real address where you would like your packages sent and make up the rest. Just be sure to remember to it as you will have to tell the merchant the same thing when you are ordering your merchandise.

Use of Business Fronts

A business front is an excellent way to keep anonymous assets such as bank accounts, vehicles, and real estate. The best kind of business to use for this is the Limited Liability Company (LLC). A LLC is almost like a corporation in that it is an entity onto itself meaning it can hold titles and deeds to property, hold accounts, and represent itself in civil court actions. You do not need nor should you use a lawyer for this as it can totally be done yourself.

To set up a LLC you will have to file an Articles of Organization along with a nominal fee with the Secretary of State. The information usually required on the articles include the name of the company (not one associated to you-duh!), the name and address of the resident agent (this can be a liaison but must be in the state you are filing in), the duration of the LLC (usually 30-50 years from the date of filing), and the address of the principal office (this can be and should be out of state). The resident agent should be a liaison and the principal office should be under an alternate address. The LLC should be filled out of the state you reside in (it's rumored that Delaware and Nevada are good choices). The regulations for LLC's vary from state to state (from easy to complex and from cheap ($10 in West Virginia) to expensive ($200 in New York). You should consult a self-help book on forming LLC's for the most current laws.

Although, illegal one could just fill out the Articles of Organization form but using a custom made rubberstamp or embossing stamp from a office supply store stating for example 'Filed with Secretary of State, December 18, 2003, by_________________' to make the form look 'certified' as if it were filed! First find out exactly what type of stamp is used in your state, have it copied and stamp your own documents. If you need to look at a sample stamp consult a lawyer or ask someone who has a LLC. The advantage of this method is it does not leave a paper trail since the real forms were never filed with the Secretary of State in the first place!

The LLC can now be used to buy vehicles such as cars, trucks, boats, and real estate anonymously if you pay cash and do not finance the purchase. When you transfer the title and sign the bill of sale or deed list the LLC as the buyer using an alternate address. To register vehicles under the LLC go to a private licensing bureau instead of the DMV. If you must use the DMV do it over the phone. Get the car insurance in your own name followed by 'd.b.a.' (doing business as) and the name of your LLC. If it's real estate give the title company a copy of the Articles of Organization with clear instructions that your name is to appear in office files only and no public databases. To maximize privacy, buy the vehicle in one state using the LLC from another state, and give an address in another state to register it. The beauty of all this is if someone does a property search or runs your license plates (including the police) the name of the LLC will show up NOT yours!

In order to get a checking account in the LLC's name, you will need to obtain an employer tax ID number (also called an EIN or TIN) by filing form SS-4 and sending it to the IRS. You will also need a business phone number, use an alternate name for this. Open a bank account at a small rural bank when it's most busy (either around lunch or closing time) with a photocopy of the LLC's Articles or Organization and give them the EIN. Use a cashier's check made to the LLC as the initial deposit. Next, advise the IRS to cancel the LLC because it will not be used. Don't worry, the LLC isn't supposed to make a profit anyway and the bank will never know. In the future endorse business checks with a rubber stamp stating 'For Deposit Only' with the LLC's name and account name. To pay bills with the checks, use a rubber stamp signature made in your's or your liaisons signature.

Using Hiding Places

How and where you hide your valuables or 'contraband' will depend on three important things. The first, what are you trying to hide? It is precious coins or jewelry, a stamp collection from the 19th century, a shitload of money, half a pound of methampthemine, a copy of 'The Satanic Verses', love letters to Bin Laden, Teflon coated bullets, a silenced rifle, photos with you and the farmer's sheep from next door, videos with you and the farmer's daughter next door, chemicals when mixed can poison half the neighborhood, or even perhaps yourself? The second is whom are you trying to hide it from? It is a burglar, nosy relatives or landlords, the police, or if you're really luckless the mafia? This is important because a two-bit thief may not be too smart, will just snatch loot what can fenced quickly (electronics, jewelry), and likes to be in and out as quickly as possible (usually ten to thirty minutes). The police on the other hand armed with a search warrant will be <u>very</u> thorough, may used special equipment (like metal detectors, x-ray machines, or ground-penetrating radar), and will have unlimited time. Lastly, if your 'stash' was found what would be the consequences- embarrassment, blackmail, loss of savings or income, arrest and prison, divorce, serious injury, or maybe even death?

Once you answered those questions you can decide how to make your hiding place. Obviously, don't use well known places- avoid anything in the bedroom including dresser drawers, closets, inside clothes pockets or socks, and under mattresses or pillows. This would the first place ANYONE would look. Likewise, avoid the medicine cabinet (many thieves are drug addicts too) and any hiding place visible from the front door of your house. .If the objects are really sensitive you may better hiding it off the premises. Perhaps you could keep it with a trusted neighbor, relative, or employer. An old drug dealer trick in New York would be to pay an old person's rent in a nearby apartment in exchange for keeping the stash of drugs in the person's place. If the police searched for drugs in the dealer's apartment they usually came up empty or with very little drugs. A search warrant only allowed them to search individual apartments not the entire building! Here's a list of ideas for possible hiding places from simple to elaborate and from small to large.

Bar of soap- Split the soap lengthwise with a warm butterknife, hollow out a cavity, insert the stash, reseal with a powerful adhesive, and using a warm knife smooth the outside edge. Also roughen the appearance of the soap.

Shaving cream can- Depress the release value ten minutes to release pressure, secure the can in a vise, open it up with a screwdriver, insert the stash, and reseal with pliers.

Stick deodorant canister- Remove the top from an empty canister and push down the platform which held the deodorant. Scrub the canister clean, let it dry, and then add your stash. Replace the canister among other toiletries.

Heels of shoes- Hollowed out from the inside.

Canned goods- Remove the label carefully. Pierce a small hole in the center of the seam. Apply heat to the seam with a mini-torch until the solder runs absorbing it with a solder wick. Pry the tin apart carefully with a screwdriver. Then with tin snips makes two small slits at the top and bottom of outside edge. Insert the stash, reseal the edges, and resolder the seam. Tidy up the rough edges with auto body repair filler and replace the label.

Toothpaste tube- Slit the bottom of the tube with a razor then using a pencil squeeze out the contents into an icing bag. Insert the stash, refill the original contents, and glue the bottom back together.

Grease gun- Place the stash at the bottom then pack the gun with grease.

Vaseline or cold cream jar- Scoop 2/3's of the contents out, insert the stash, and then heat the scooped out contents and pour it back in the jar.

Paint cans, creosote, or any other thick, opaque liquid- Seal the stash in a heavy plastic bag with weights inside to insure it stinks to the bottom.

Postal system- Pack the item well, seal it in a plastic bag, and wrap it with paper designed to protect film from X-ray's. Insure the package too for good measure.

Bicycle pump- Remove the piston assembly from the inside, shorten the rod, and insert the stash.

Pottery or clay ashtrays, mugs, or teapots- Insert the stash in the clay prior to molding the pottery.

Soccer ball- Using a sharp knife, cut along the sides of the patches and open it like a flap. Insert the stash and secure it with tape. Then resew the flap and apply a thin layer of clear cement.

Face sponge- Cut it into two sections, hollow out a cavity into the lower section, insert the stash, and reseal. Then, doctor the sponge with bits of dirt, old soap, and pubic hair to deter handling.

Polystyrene packaging- Using a blade cut a slice and cut out a cavity. Insert the stash, replace the slice, and secure with polystyrene cement.

Casted bricks- Construct a wooden mold modeled on a real brick. Pour in plaster of paris or cement half way, put in the stash, and pour in the rest of the plaster or cement. Be sure to seal the stash in heavy plastic bags and it must NOT be heat sensitive.

Loaf of bread- Make a cavity inside the middle of the loaf, insert the stash, and rewrap the bread.

Flowerpots or window boxes- Very well known but it still works. Make a false bottom in the pot or box, insert the stash, replace the flowers and soil on top.

Box of cornflakes- Carefully open the inside bag, pour out the cornflakes, insert the stash, and pour the cornflakes back inside.

Drainpipe- Lift the cover, attach a string to the stash and the cover. Drop the stash down the pipe, and replace the cover.

Aquarium-Best used if it has dangerous fish like piranhas or electric eels and hide the stash inside the gravel.

Refrigerator/ freezer panel- Wear gloves to protect against the insulation inside first. Then unscrew the panel, insert the stash, rescrew, and clean up the area.

Food- Hide the stash inside half gallon tubs of butter, bags of flour or sugar, baked cakes and pies, stuffed turkeys, ice cream, jars of peanut butter, mayonnaise, cooking fat, smelly foods (fish), sour milk, fruit juice, or a block of ice.

Button badge- Using a 'badge-a-mint' machine, insert the stash between the paper button and the metal part.

Picture frame- Take out the board behind, lay the stash flat in the frame, and put the board back on.

Record album- If the stash is flat or thin, take a crappy album that noone is likely to listen or steal for that matter and put it inside the record sleeve.

Homemade candle– Using a glass jar or other mold pour in paraffin wax (melted on a double boiler) halfway, insert your stash (protected in plastic), pour in the remainder of the wax and let it cool.

Large bag of dry dog food or kitty litter- Empty out the contents, place stash on the bottom of the bag, and pour the contents back in.

Base of lamp– Open up the base of a lamp, insert the stash, and close the base

Dummy electrical socket- Buy a socket box, socket, and face plate at the hardware store. Cut out a hole in the sheetrock with a keyhole saw, screw the box to a stud, insert stash, and put on the faceplate.

Range hood filter- Remove the filter from the hood, put in the stash, and replace the filter. The filter should not look clean and new. Best to use a grease caked nasty filter to deter any handling.

Toilet tank- Remove the cover from the tank, tape the stash to the cover, and replace the cover. For extra security put something HEAVY on top of the toilet tank.

Pillows, stuffed animals, toys, dolls- Neatly cut a slit in one of these, remove enough of the stuffing to make room for your stash, insert the stash, pad the excess space with stuffing, and neatly resew the object.

Hardcover book- Open the book and leaf through a third of the pages. Then with a utility knife and a ruler cut a square hollow from the center of the remaining second third of the pages. Remove the cut out section and glue the pages together inside of the square opening. Let the book dry and tape your stash inside.

Electric baseboard heater- If the stash isn't flammable or heat sensitive this can be used. Make sure the heater is unplugged, remove the cover, insert your stash, and then replace the cover.

Wall clock- Open up the back of the clock with a screwdriver, insert the stash, and replace the back.

Vacuum cleaner bag- This is good to use on a non-functioning vacuum cleaner. Find a bag that fits the vacuum cleaner, put in your stash, fill the bag with crap (dust bunnies, dirt, whatever), and put the bag on the vacuum cleaner.

Birdhouse- If your handy with tools you can build a birdhouse with a removable top and put it the backyard.

Insulation- Wearing gloves, peel backs the flaps of insulation, tape in the stash, and replace the flap.

Compost pile- The stinkier, the better- place the stash in a heavy plastic bag, duct tape it shut, and place it as far as possible inside. Some good sized roadkill can be placed inside the compost as well to attract files, maggots, and other vermin to deter any searching.

Furniture- Cut a square opening in fabric underneath in a chair or couch, hide stash within the padding, and resew the opening very carefully.

Mirror on door- Make a hollow behind a full length mirror on the closet door then mount the mirror on sliding tabs.

Table or desk- Remove the molding and make a hollow, place in the stash, and replace the molding.

Hollow core door- Cut a slot at the top, drop in the goods, and then fill the slot with wood putty.

Clothes hamper- Empty out clothes, place stash at bottom, and replace clothes.

False roof vent– Buy a roof ventilator, attach it to the roof, and put your stash inside.

Mattress, boxspring, or zippered cushion– Neatly cut an opening in the mattress or box-spring fabric, put in the stash, and carefully resew the opening. With the cushion, just unzip the zipper, put in the stash, and rezip it.

Walls- Hollow out behind solid, fixed items (coat racks, boards)

Dog house or rabbit hutch- Hide the stash inside or under the roof of any of these.

Spare Tire- Deflate the tire, put in the goods, put air back in it, and stow the tire.

Baseboards- Remove away a section from the wall, hollow out an area between the studs, insert stash, and tack back the section in place neatly.

Acoustic tile ceiling- If you have acoustic tiles ceilings, simply remove a tile or two put in the stash, and replace the tiles.

Dummy air conditioner- Install a broken down air conditioner in the window, remove the faceplate, pull the internal unit, and discard.

Place the stash in the empty shell and replace the face with buttons and knobs intact.

Dummy ductwork/ plumbing/ stovepipe- Either buy plumbing stock from the hardware store and install it going across the basement or better look for existing connections and add sealed dummies to them.

Dummy air intake- Cut a hole into sheetrock of the wall with a keyhole saw or a router, insert a metal box and screw it to a stud, insert the stash, and cover the box with a faceplate.

Dummy beams- Ceiling and walls

Wall paneling– If your stash is thin and flat you can measure and cut paneling to a wall, attach the stash to the inside of the paneling, and then nail the paneling to the wall. You can even add baseboards and or molding if you wish.

Dummy hot water heater or washing machine- Take an old non-working heater or washer, put in dummy pipes into the plumbing, and hide the stash inside.

Wooded Areas- Inside stump of old redwood trees

Abandoned buildings- Inside old shafts, culverts, broken walls, loose floorboards, weed thickets

Underground- Bury the stash in 4"-8" diameter PVC water pipes. You will need PVC pipe, an end cap, a screwtop end, PVC pipe cement, Teflon sealing tape, and a hacksaw. First cut the pipe down to the right size with the hacksaw. Then, prepare the surface on the end of the pipe with steel wool, apply PVC cement and stick the end cap on one end. Do the same to the other end with the screw top end. Allow the cement to set for 24 hours. Drive out the moisture by turning the oven to its lowest temperature (this VERY important- PVC is plastic) for 15 minutes and take the pipe out. Prepare the stash by putting it in a sealed heavy duty bag with 2 oz. of desiccant (such as silca gel) in a sock. If the stash is metal wrap it in cheesecloth, sit it overnight in a dry oven at 250 degrees, apply a coat of oil to it, wrap it in aluminum foil or waxpaper, and then put it in a ziplock baggie with desiccant in a sock. Put in your stash, place Teflon tape on the threads, and screw the end on. Bury the pipe vertically 3 feet deep and cover with 18 inches of dirt then place a part from the auto scrap yard like an alternator or carb in the hole and fill the hole. The auto scrap hopefully will act as a decoy for any wiseass deciding to use a metal detector. Burying the goods under an old abandoned car or refrigerator is another possibility. For best results, bury more scrap metal randomly around the area and at different depths. A variation of this is to bury the goods next to a fence. Dig a hole next to the fence with a post digger and drop in a sealed pvc pipe with the goods. The fence will act as a decoy for the metal detector.

Secret room- Install a metal or solid wood door with two deadbolts and line the interior with plywood.

Private rental storage facility- This is probably the best way to hide contraband from the police besides burying it. Rent out a storage place in another town or state using a liaison or an alternate name (NEVER use your real name) and pay cash several months in advance for it.

Dealing with the Police

Under the U.S. Constitution there are aspects of the law that in theory protect your 'Individual Liberties'. Unfortunately, the law presumes you know them and if you don't it's very easy to waive them, as the police are experts in tricking the ignorant and the intimidated to do exactly that. Police are there to 'protect and serve' in theory only. In reality, many will follow or bend the letter of the law while ignoring the sprit of the law. Many will do anything they want and will lie about it later. In my opinion, there are no good cops only bad ones and worse and not to be trusted ever. However, if they think you know your rights all but the worst cops will probably ease up on you.

First, make sure you are dealing with a real police officer as criminals are increasingly impersonating them. Ask for identification from any non-uniformed person claiming to be an officer. If you're in a car and the people trying to stop you are really the police but with no lightbar, no marked car, and no uniforms– turn on your flashers and keep driving at a safe speed to the nearest police/ fire station or open gas station. If more police cars appear stop immediately. They will NOT be happy about this but given the times they should understand your behavior. Always keep your hands in plain sight on the steering wheel and your arms at your sides, make no sudden moves, and speak in a level, calm voice. Be polite and to the point but firm at the same time. If you are stopped at night– pull off the road, turn off the ignition, lock your doors, put up all windows except the driver's, and turn on the overhead light. Do not reach into your pockets, bag, or glove compartment unless told to do so. Do NOT get out your car unless told to do so as they will perceive this as a threat. If you're on the street and are stopped keep your hands visible and open. Do not reach into your pockets or bags unless told to do so. Avoid walking behind them. Never touch them or their equipment. This stuff makes cops nervous and nervous cops are dangerous cops. You may be beaten and charged with resisting arrest or assault. If they panic they might do something real drastic, like shoot you!

They are three types of police/citizen contacts– consensual contact or conversation, detention, and arrest. You must know the difference between these because if you are not careful a consensual contact or a detention could easily turn into an arrest. If an officer comes to you and says 'Can I speak with you?', do NOT say yes. If you do you have 'consented' to have contact with the police and thus waive various rights under the law. NEVER consent to talk to the police. Especially if you think you may be guilty of something (warrant, carrying contraband, or just did something illegal) and even if you don't it is still not a good idea to voluntarily speak with them. They may not have enough evidence for a detention or arrest so they'll try to get the information they need from you. If they ask to speak with you say 'I'm sorry, I'm in a hurry and don't have time to talk now.' If you're on the street walk away or at home shut the door. If he insists, ask him 'Are you detaining me? Am I free to leave?' Ask several times if you have to, to reduce the chance the officer might lie and say you didn't mention it if it goes to court. If it's really a consensual contact the officer should just let you go on your way. If you do not ask verbally if you can leave, the court will presume you have consented to have contact with the police.

The next step up the ladder is detention. Which is basically, even though you're not under arrest you can't leave. An officer can only detain you when they are 'specific and articulable facts supporting suspicion' (SAF) or reasonable suspicion you are involved in criminal activity. This doesn't mean a 'hunch', it means they must have observed something about your behavior or character links you with specific criminal activity. In theory– if they detain you without SAF, the detention is illegal and whatever they obtain as a result (evidence or an arrest) is inadmissable in court. Now in practice (or the real world)– what if the police stop you because you are out late at night, loitering, look 'funny', homeless, gay, the wrong ethnicity, or they're just having a bad day? Ask them 'Am I being detained?' If they say no just walk away and say nothing else to them. If they say yes ask them why. Then say these magic words "I am going to remain silent, until I see a lawyer" and say nothing else. It is crucial that you let them know you are NOT consenting to talk to them. SAF may exist in some circumstances like if you fit the description of a suspect in a recent crime or if they show up and you start running. If they have SAF the detention isn't illegal but this can't be just anything, the facts have to be very specific. Lots of arrests happen because the police stop people who look 'wrong' and go on fishing expeditions looking for a valid rationale for an arrest which they didn't have at first. The police detain people for two reasons 1) they want to issue a citation (like a ticket) or 2) they want to arrest you but don't have enough evidence to do so yet. Many detentions turn into arrests because the person talked too much, physically resisted, was found with drugs or weapons, or had a warrant. Don't give them a chance– if they want to talk with you, just say NO! Be polite but don't volunteer information about persons or incidents no matter what they promise or threaten. Anything you say can be taken out of context and used against you. Provide only your name, identification, and registration (if it's a traffic stop) then say the magic words "I am going to be silent, until I see a lawyer."

Many people will try to lie to the police. This is NOT advisable; it is a crime to lie to the police. Unfortunately, the police (especially undercovers) are permitted to lie to you if they think you're involved in a crime. Yes, undercovers don't have to tell you they are police. They are even permitted to commit crimes and do drugs with you if it means getting a conviction. Moreover, people lie to the police all the time and they can be very good at detecting conflicting stories and facts. It is better to stay silent. However, if you decide to give them false information- be consistent! Know how to spell your alias and sign it right. If you give a false date of birth, know the zodiac sign. A shrewd cop will sometimes ask your sign if he suspects you're giving him a bullshit date of birth. Also be sure to memorize any false past addresses by heart.

If the police ask to search you or your car without arresting you, do NOT consent to a search. Ask if you are under arrest or if they have a warrant. No arrest, no warrant, no consent to search. Tell them "I do not consent to this search", if they ask several times– just say NO. They do have the right to frisk you, look inside your car or the immediate area in a detention if they suspect you may be armed but nothing else like your pockets, bags, or the car trunk unless you give your consent. If you are armed surrender the weapon voluntarily before the search. But you must tell them you do not consent to a search. If you don't object, consent will be presumed and the search will be legal. Unfortunately, the police trick people into consenting by making a request sound like an order or not even asking and hoping you're ignorant enough not to notice. If they ask, they probably don't have the right to search and need your consent. If they search anyway, politely but firmly state you don't consent to the search but don't physically resist them either. A warning in car stops, if they decide to use a dog to sniff - it CAN establish probable cause!! By the way the warrantless auto search rules can apply to ANY mobile vehicle; including houseboats, airplanes, buses, towed and impounded vehicles, or even train roomettes- the key word here is mobile. Remember and write down names of officers, badge numbers, name of witnesses, and details so you can file a compliant later. If you have a digital voice recorder, consider discreetly making a recording of the contact. One caution though, police don't like people taking notes especially if they're doing something they shouldn't doing. They may get more aggressive but it may prevent them from abusing you.

If the police arrive at your home do not invite them inside nor should you step outside. If they believe you committed a felony, usually they will need an arrest warrant to go into the house to arrest. Don't make it easy for them by stepping outside. If they ask you to step outside tell them 'I am comfortable right here, what do you need?', 'No you may not come in.', 'Do you have a warrant to enter or arrest in my home?'. No officer has the right to enter your home or arrest you without just cause or a warrant. Again they may try to make their request an informal order. Ask them 'Are they asking you or ordering you?' They may try to threaten you or bargain with you. You may be asked, "What do you have to hide?" turn it around and say "What type of question is that?" They may threaten to trash the house later if you don't consent to a search and force them to get a warrant. In any search this usually happens anyway so have nothing to lose by not consenting to a warrantless search. If they are real assholes they may even threaten to take children and pets away later if you don't consent. Even if they have to leave and come back with a warrant you have brought an important asset– time. It is crucial that EVERYONE (even kids and guests) on the property understand not to any circumstances to consent to a search if the police come. Some sneaky lowdown cops have been known to trick children into giving consent. Put up a note next to the door if you have to. In addition if you rent check your lease, some have clauses allowing the landlord to authorize consent **whether you agree to it or not**! If they do have a warrant, still refuse to consent to a search and ask to read the warrant. You have nothing to lose by refusing to consent and if the warrant happens to incorrect or invalid the search will be illegal. When reading the warrant it must have; a recent date (usually within 1-2 weeks), the correct address and apartment number (if there is one), and the judge's or magistrate' signature. The correct address is important as it isn't uncommon for cops to bust in the door on the wrong residence. If they have a search warrant and it is correct you will have no choice but to let them serach. Then immediately call a lawyer and be sure to observe and document everything (videotape them if possible). If you have a friend in the press call them too. A search warrant is supposed to be used to gather evidence for an indictment. If no indictment is forthcoming demand any property seized to be returned and file suit. Even if you don't win, it might teach these pricks some manners. Now they are some just causes (not in my opinion though) for the police to conduct a warrantless search. These include you giving consent (you would never do that now.. eh), the immediate area following an arrest, anything illegal seen in 'plain view' (don't keep bongs out in the open!), impounded vehicles (even for tow away zones), pursuit of a fleeing suspect, a fire or rescue, or when someone may be in immediate danger (a cry for help, sounds of a fight or gunfire). Also anyone under court supervision (probation, parole, house arrest) frequently has to submit to warrantless searches as a condition of their release. If you are under court supervision it might be a good idea to read those release papers NOW! In addition, anyone boarding an airplane, anyone crossing the border, and many students in high school are subject to warrantless searches of their person and belongings.

Now if the police say you are under arrest they must have probable cause. This means they are aware of facts that would lead an ordinary person to suspect that the person arrested has committed a crime. Once you are under arrest they can search you, your belongings, or your vehicle (even the trunk). If a strip search is conducted the officer doing the searching must be of the same gender. If you are presented with an arrest warrant at your home, close the door and do NOT go back into the house for any reason nor accept any offers to do so. If you do they are allowed to search any room you go into without a warrant. If you need to secure your house call a friend to do it later. You may or may not be read your rights (as known as the Miranda Warning). If you are under arrest do NOT run, do NOT physically resist, and keep silent.

The two sentences in the Miranda Warning states "You have to right to remain silent. Anything you say can and will be used against you in a court of law." This means **exactly** what it says!! People under arrest fuck up here more than anywhere else. Once you have been arrested, don't try to talk yourself out of it– it's useless. Don't try to proclaim your innocence or make excuses. Nothing you say will prevent you from being booked and anything you say can be used against you. The police don't decide guilt and really don't care since it's the job of the judge or jury to decide guilt or innocence. Save your defense for your attorney. Remember, you have the right to be silent– use it!! Don't have any dialogue with the police whatsoever. Don't respond to any accusations, any questions, any threats, nothing. Even if you're innocent keep silent– your statement may be misunderstood, misquoted, and sometimes outright distorted. Don't get friendly or have conversations or small talk with them. Assume any interaction will be recorded without your knowledge and used against you. They may be trying to get information from you. They may tell you they have enough information to convict you. But they will promise 'to go easy on you' if you would just confess. This is a trick, if they have enough to convict why are they talking to you? Beware of the good cop/ bad cop ruse. It may be the oldest trick in the book but many normally intelligent people happen to fall for it. Frequently, they can and will lie about evidence and even create false documents. They will sometimes separate two co-consiprators in order to get them to 'rat' on each other. Don't believe them for a second, it's just a trap. If you know you're guilty and want to make a deal, talk **directly** to and get a written agreement from the prosecutor with your lawyer present and **no one** else. The prosecution is the only one in authority to honor any 'deals.' Your only response to any questions (besides your name and address– give them your alternate address) should be "I going to remain silent, until I see a lawyer." Don't make any decisions about case before seeing a lawyer either. Once a lawyer becomes involves, police lose much of their power to intimidate. In fact, get in a habit of carrying the business card of a local criminal attorney in your wallet or purse at all times. Only a judge can order you to answer questions. Never sign anything unless you know exactly what it is means. Usually signing a promise to appear in court is ok to sign. If you are asked to sign a property receipt form, read it very carefully before signing. Never sign waiver of rights, a statement, or a merchant confession form. Be careful what you say and do in the police vehicle and jail cells. They may have video and audio recorders. Also fellow prisoners (who may be snitches) and jailers can be called as witnesses to testify on conversations you had even if just overheard. When you are able to make your phone call– do not talk about the incident, anything illegal, or even other people. The phone call may be monitored. Discuss arrangements for your lawyer or bail only.

Use of Disguises

In a situation where you want to escape recognition the use of disguise may be necessary. This can be very simple to quite elaborate depending on your needs. All the techniques here can be done by anyone with some practice. All of these methods are designed for temporary purposes only. Therefore, any plastic surgery type alterations like facelifts, nose and chin jobs, hair transplants, tummy tucks, skin bleaching (think Michael Jackson), etc. which are permanent are beyond the scope of this book and not included.

First you need to be aware of ways people identify others. Some researchers have determined these six main qualities:

Hair- Style, length, color, quantity

Face- Hair (beard, mustache, goatee, sideburns), physical characteristics (eyes, nose, lips, teeth, ears), glasses, makeup, piercings, jewelry, wrinkles

Clothes- Style, type, color, texture, shoes

Body- Ethnicity, gender, height, weight, body type, posture, disabilities

Gait- Walking, standing, running

Accessories- Jewelry (belt buckles, rings, bracelets), pipe or cigarettes, cane, crutches, briefcase, purse, backpack, cellphone, pager

Next ask two friends (one male, one female) and two strangers (again one male, one female) what they think are your ten most identifying characteristics. The usage of friends and strangers as well as two genders is important. Strangers may focus on characteristics that your friends may have long forgotten about due to the 'first impressions' factor. Men and women tend to perceive things differently. Men tend to notice general characteristics while many women will be more specific noticing things that most men would completely miss! Now you have a list of forty identifying characteristics (some may be the same). After reviewing this list carefully, your goal should be to dress and behave completely opposite to what is on that list.

Sometimes the best disguise is just dress to blend in. This can be as simple as wearing overralls and a hardhat, a Hawaiian shirt and a tourist hat, a suit and a briefcase, or coveralls and a toolbox depending upon your environment. Some stereotypes are more visible than others and leave a more lasting impression upon the human mind. Stereotypes that tend to be very visible include prostitutes, hippies, bikers, clergypeople, tourists, people of different ethnicity than the area, musicians, punk rockers, pregnant women, police officers, doctors, and homeless people. Invisible stereotypes tend to include servants, waiters, housewives, construction workers, repair people, business people, mail people, college students, delivery people, and senior citizens. Remember though- environment is very important. A person dressed as a punk at a rock concert or a homeless person at a soup kitchen would fit right in while a suit and tie person would stick out completely!

Minor props also known as detractors because their main purpose is to draw attention away from other characteristics can be used to aid in a disguise. These include roll-up hats, brightly colored coats, loud t-shirts, eyeglasses, sunglasses, mirrored lenses, colored contacts, eyepatches, flashy jewelry, clip on piercings, temporary tattoos, gold tooth caps, or false teeth. Hair dyes (like Clariol, L'oreal) and bleaches can make a brunette go to a redhead, a blonde to a brunette, a mousy to platinum, and so on. Varying hairstyles for example crewcuts, braids, spiked, mohawk, dreadlocks, or long hair are simple and easy to change. Natural disguises such as mustaches can hide a long upper lip, growing a beard can hide a weak chin or a thin face, and dieting to gain or lose weight can change the body profile. The main disadvantage with natural disguises is that they take time to be effective.

A fake hairpiece like wigs, mustaches, and sideburns is what most people think of normally when you say 'disguise'. Wigs can be brought at a beauty parlor or a department store where you can select one for a match in color, texture of hair, and proper fit. Use an adhesive to hold it on and make sure it has a net backing made of elastic. Mustaches and sideburns can be brought at novelty shops. Hold it against your face as you want it to fit then cut off the excess hair, if necessary. When finished apply spirit gum to clean, dry skin and to the lace side of the hairpiece, let the gum get tacky, and use a cloth to press the hairpiece firmly to the skin. To remove it press a cloth moistened with acetone or rubbing alcohol against it. There is also wool crepe hair which is more realistic for the face but more difficult to work with. Professional actors tend to use this mostly. It is sold in braids, which you pull out and separate to the desired thickness. It is applied the same way as other hairpieces with spirit gum and can be trimmed when the glue dries. Use hairspray to keep any hairpiece in shape and not require constant combing.

Other aids can be used to alter the appearance. Padded clothing can give the illusion of a 'pot belly.' Shoe lifts or a tall hat can conceal one's true height. Tanning lotions such as Man-Tan or Bonne-Bel darkens the skin, although it streaks with water. Placing a pebble in one show can stimulate a limping walk. In addition, using a cane or crutches will enhance this image. A broken arm can be stimulated by wearing a sling and walking slightly sideways so as to guard the arm. A missing tooth can be stimulated by cleaning the tooth first with a paper towel then molding and applying a black tooth wax. This will be however visible upon close inspection. Colored tooth enamels can stimulate brown, decayed, or nicotine stained teeth. There is also a product called Eyeblood which colors the eyes for bloodshot or jaundiced eyes effect. Good sources for these and makeup (discussed later) are available online at Stagesupply.com, Graftobian.com, and Kryolan.com.

Disguising the voice can be useful because many people remember voice differences acutely. People can tell region, gender, ethnicity, amount of education, and other differences by speech. Placing a marble under the tongue or using false plates will change the position of the tongue and therefore change the voice. You can also put earplugs on so you'll talk louder and stress hi-pitch sounds like s and z to change your voice. To create a deeper voice use nose plugs or cotton in your cheeks. To imitate hoarseness speak in a loud whisper. You can alter your speech pattern by introducing grammatical errors, mispronunciations, and punctuate sentences with certain words. To imitate accents you will need a recording of a person of the same gender speaking in the accent you wish to simulate. Then practice, practice, and practice some more as you test your progress with a voice recorder. Practicing accents is very important because a native's ears are much attuned to the real thing.

If you're from New York, practice a southern accent a few times and try to say you're from the south- it may fool other New Yorkers but don't try it with someone from Georgia!

Fingerprints can be disguised as well. First method involves brushing the fingers sandpaper then coating them with thin layer of airplane glue or spaying the fingers with clear lacquer or lacquer based hair spray. Second method (called dermabrasion) which is more ...er uncomfortable involves using a drum sander to carefully remove the top layer of the skin. This will remove the ridges that make fingerprints and will leave smooth fingertips. The ridges will grow back in a few weeks but since having ridges helps us grip things and do activities requiring fine hand dexterity– picking up, catching objects, typing, and the like will be more difficult.

Make-up can be used to suppress identifying scars or blemishes, change facial features, or create false blemishes. A good makeup kit for disguise will include cream foundation (various shades), a cake of translucent face powder, blush (pale pink, maroon, brown), eyeshadow (various shades), eyeliner pencils, a bottle of liquid latex, a tube of molding wax, spirit gum, a tube of hair whitener, cleansing cream, various sizes of brushes, a large sponge, and a mirror. A good department store and theatrical makeup store should have these. Stick with good brands like Revlon or Max Factor and test it on your face before you buy.

If you're a guy and never used make-up before you should enlist the help of a woman or transgender friend to help you apply it correctly. Basically, the foundation is applied first on the cheeks, nose, chin, and forehead with a damp sponge sparingly and then blended over the face. It is upon this that eyeshadow, blush, and other makeup is blended into. Use only a small amount of makeup at a time. Blend it in and avoid clobs. Check the facial hair for flecks of makeup and then blot the face with a lightly amp towel.

To cover scars and blemishes use a foundation close to your skin tone. Apply it with your fingers blending it into the skin at edges of the area you're covering, and then cover it with a light coat of face powder. If you have deep pits, first coat your fingers with K-Y lubricating jelly or a light coat of cleansing cream (NOT

Vaseline) and fill them in with molding wax. Then feather the edges to blend it with the skin and cover with foundation.

To create a wart on the nose wet your fingers with K-Y lubricating jelly and break off an ample amount of molding wax. Apply it to the spot on your nose you want to build up then carefully shape and blend it in with the contours of the nose. Blend from the inside out so as to get thin of a layer as possible outside. If you have trouble having the wax stick sometimes applying some spirit gum to the skin can help. Apply cream foundation and face powder if the wax doesn't match.

If you want to create a scar build up a line using liquid latex or molding wax. Then mold it until you have the type of scar you want. It should be uneven as real scars are or V shaped like surgical scars. Slice the scar down the middle, fill the crack with dark eyeshadow, and blend it in.

Creating bruises is easy, just mottle violet-blue or lavender eyeshadow powder on the skin and then add it deeper at the center. The colors should be blended and mixed to resemble a real bruise. A black eye uses the same method just the bruising is done around the eyes.

Creating burns is more intricate, you first apply two thin coats of latex to the area to be treated letting each layer dry before applying the next. Try not to wrinkle the skin while waiting for it to dry. When the layers have dried apply a light coat of face powder and layer it with a sunburn shade of cream foundation. Lift up a section of the layer of latex with a pair of tweezers. Cut out the center of this section. Then, peel back the edges and apply some cream foundation of a slightly redder shade in the hole.

If you want to stimulate aging, make a face so the wrinkles in your face show then enhance them by lightly drawing soft eyeliner pencil in brown, maroon, or gray at the bottom of each wrinkle. Subtly shade blue-gray eyeshadow under the eyes and blush darker than your normal skin color on the cheeks and temples. In addition, prior to using makeup you could apply liquid latex or Kryolan Old Skin Plast. It is brush upon stretched skin around the eyes, cheeks, and forehead then upon releasing the skin makes it look wrinkled. Finally, use hair whitener on the eyebrows, wear a gray wig, and line the hands to help the illusion. Similarly stimulating a sickly appearance can be done by using a light colored foundation on the face and blue-gray or purplish eyeshadow under the eyes.

If you really want to go for the low-life look you can even make needle tracks. Spread a thin layer of Elmers glue in a line half an inch long following a line of vein causing the skin to wrinkle. When the glue dries, brush on blue-gray, brown, and maroon shades of eyeliner pencil or eyeshadow. Keep the color irregular and shade it into the surrounding skin.

Using theatrical makeup effectively takes patience and practice for the inexperienced person. If you're interested in seriously studying this further I suggest reading two excellent books. They are both called Stage Makeup but they are two different books, one is written by Richard Corson and the other is by Rosemarie Swinfield.

Defeating Drug Testing

A very disturbing business dealing with urine is going on these days. It's not enough that the powers that be want your mind and soul but they want your urine too. Who in their right mind would want someone else's urine?? I sure wouldn't!! However, on a serious note drug testing is an increasing way for corporate and government masters to control their subjects.

Typically, there are basically four methods for defeating drug testing; abstinence, flushing, substitution, and contamination. Obviously the best way is abstinence from <u>all</u> drugs including prescription and over-the-counter some of which can cause false positives. The drugs they test for have a certain detection limit, which is how long you have to avoid the drug to be clean. The limits are presented on a table below. These limits can vary from person to person so double or triple these times to be safe.

Amphetamines	2-4 days
Alcohol	12-24 hours

Barbiturates/ Quaaludes	2-4 days
Heroin, Opium	2-4 days
Tranquilizers	Up to 30 days
PCP (light use)	2-7 days
Cocaine	12-72 hours
PCP (heavy use)	Up to 1 month
Pot (light use)	2-7 days
LSD	20-40 days
Pot (heavy use)	1-2 months (!!)

These are some over-the-counter or prescription drugs that can give false positives.

Ibuprofen (Advil, Nuprin, Mortin) for Pot
Cold and asthma medicines (Diatec, Dexatrim, Co-Tylenol, Triaminic, Primatine, Brunkotabs, Nyquil)
for Amphetamines
Vicks 44, Demerol, Mydol, Primatene-M, and antidepressants like Elavil and Tofani for Opium and Heroin
Primatine for Barbiturates
Benadryl for Methadone
Other medicines to avoid include Alka-seitzer plus, Allerest, Bronkaid, Contac, Donnagel, Sinutab, and Sudafed.

You can also reduce the concentration of drugs in your urine by flushing. This is flushing as much liquid through the body as possible. Usually, drinking lots of water, tea, coffee, and colas plus urinating as much as possible. In case your urine looks overly clear which may make them suspicious take lots of vitamin C. This will make your urine dark yellow. If possible, a doctor maybe able to prescribe Lasix which is a powerful diuretic; which is something that'll have you pissing like a racehorse. A couple other substances that are said to work are cranberry juice, vinegar, and golden seal but their effectiveness is skeptical. Large amounts of antioxidants such as vitamins A, C, and E which help your body get rid of waste may help as well.

Another method which is substitution involves switching your dirty urine with someone else's that is clean. The strategy behind this can get quite difficult depending on how closely you are watched when you are tested. Another problem is that you have to make sure that the clean urine is really clean. If I switched my urine with most of my buddies it might test positive for anything! This is when having straight edge friends comes in handy. Don't even try the yellow food coloring in water or the dog urine trick. They are very wise to both. A product you may consider is 'Urine Luck' which claims that adding their vial to your urine will render it clean. They can be reached at 1-800-721-1414. Now you need a container to sneak in the clean urine. It has to be an easily hidden plastic bag such as double bagged condoms or a special bag from a medical supply store. Two more things- the urine cannot be more than 48 hours old (after that it deteriorates which'll be noticed in a lab test) and it should be kept warm so it seems fresh. Some places even take the temperature of the urine after they you!!

The final method is contamination, adding something to your urine that will screw up the test. One popular one is a little salt mixed with the urine. While it works on the cheap tests, other more sophisticated tests check the pH balance and too much salt will cause the pH to go outside the normal range for urine. Also the salt has to be completely dissolved. Having salt floating in the cup is a dead giveaway. Other contaminants that are reputed to work are two tablespoons of bleach or a capful of ammonia. Obviously, this has two problems- the smell and the color. Hydrogen peroxide supposedly has the same effect but without the smell problem. Another tactic is to use an IV bag with saline solution like the ones in the hospitals. Most drugstores will carry them. One could tape the bag under the arm and run the tubes down to the crotch. Another plus is that the saline is undetectable and you won't have the undissolved salt problem.

FRUGAL LIVING

The lack of a living wage, the shifting of the tax burden from the rich to the lower and middle classes, outsourcing of jobs, and the rising costs of health care are but a few of the reasons of the increased interest in frugal living. Or as I like to call it the art of drinking champagne on a beer budget. Through intelligent and shrewd purchasing decisions and an anti-consumerist state of mind it is possible to live well on less money. Many people equate frugal with cheap or poor but this is not true. It is not just for the indigent, underemployed, or debt strapped, even if you are well off living frugally can help you save money for your senior years or an emergency. As the old saying goes a penny saved is a penny earned. Other frugal living writers shy away from illegal or 'unethical' techniques but I won't. While the Walmarts and other cutthroat corporations of the world engage in what was called sharp business practices. I will show you some sharp frugal living practices. Use them at your own risk.

One of the main two goals is to reduce your spending of money for goods and services. The principal ways to do this is to follow the five R's (repair it, renew it, reduce it, reuse it, and recycle it). Think if you can you buy it cheaper or used, rent it, borrow it, or make it before buying anything new. Don't pay retail unless absolutely necessary, buy it wholesale or used first. Try garage sales, auctions, thrift and consignment stores, street vendors, eBay, or Craigslist for good secondhand deals. Some of the best stuff to get from these places includes books, cookware, dishes, toys, clothing, bedding, jewelry, decor, sporting goods, school and craft supplies, furniture, appliances, videos, music, pet supplies, tools, and outdoor gear. At garage sales you can haggle the price, if it's still too expensive loop back after it's over and you may get it for free. If want some upscale bargains in book collections, good furniture, or art and sculpture go to an estate sale. The Chinese had an old saying, taste ten times before swallowing. You should shop the same way, comparison shop at ten stores before making a purchase. Use coupons, rebates, and sales whenever possible. If you're paying cash you may be able to negotiate a lower price, try it all they can say is no. Don't upgrade electronics or appliances unless it's necessary not just because it's new. Rent or borrow, don't buy items you will seldom use. Avoid buying disposable goods such as paper towels, paper napkins, paper utensils, paper plates (you can snatch these at fast food places for free) - what are trying to do overflow a landfill? Watch less TV and you'll want fewer things. Live Spartan and minimalist- less stuff= less maintenance= less money to spend. One last thing, once you buy something- always use it up! Don't throw out what's left in the container. Turn bottles upside down to drain the last bit, tear open sugar and flour sacks, and cut open the box to get the bag of wine. Reminding yourself that whatever you're thinking of buying will cost in working hours (1, 10, or 100) will make you more aware of the cash you spend.

Living Debt Free

'The rich rule over the poor and the borrower becomes the lender's slave.' Proverbs 22:7. Being a god damned atheist I'm not much a fan of biblical quotes however this one makes perfect sense. To truly live frugal you must avoid all debt which is the second main goal! If you have never gotten a credit card- don't ever get one it is a trap. To further emphasize this I'm going to tell you a little history lesson. Credit cards are a product of the twentieth century first appearing in the 1950's originally for the upper class. Then by the 1960's they were being offered to the working and middle classes to 'free' them of the restraints of having to use cash to buy goods and services by allowing them to use money they haven't earned yet. The corporations offering credit cards made their profits through interest rates. In the past the interest rates in most states were capped but now due to government deregulation most states allow unlimited interest rates. For corporations issuing credit cards it is tantamount to a license to steal from the unsuspecting consumer. The nest step, they reduced the minimum monthly payment that a debtor must make. For example if you were paying a minimum of 5% of your balance you owed they cut it to 2%. Before you would pay $50 for every $1,000 you owed them. Now you can owe $2,500 and still would have to pay only $50. However, you would owe the money for a longer period of time (years maybe even decades instead of months) and those corporations made more profit from the unlimited interest rates. The final step was to invent new fees- late fees, over the limit fees, annual fees, process fees, balance transfer fees, and the infamous universal default fee. This vile fee allows them to raise your interest rate for any payment that is late and it doesn't even have to be to their credit card!! And believe me they have hired legions of attorneys and MBA's to dream up more fees. Presently, the United States has a consumer debt toppling a whopping $1 trillion! Bankruptcy is at an all time high, so bad the government passed new regulations making it more difficult to declare chapter 13. Don't even let me get started on the predatory mortgage lending and home foreclosure crisis!! There's an epidemic of college students in debt due to aggressive marketing by credit card companies no doubt taking advantage of student's naïveté about credit. Our instant gratification buy now, pay later attitude in society has Americans literally addicted to credit like crack cocaine. Avoid credit at ALL costs, it is a trap, the most expensive way to buy anything, and in my opinion legal robbery. Although my main target is credit cards other kinds of debt such as monthly installment plans, car loans, and student loans can be just as bad. Car loans should be avoided because a new car depreciates the minute you drive it off the lot and with their interest rates so high by the time the loan is paid off you probably paid for the car two times over. Leasing a car is a pretty much waste of money as well. Student loans can be bad too. You can by dumb luck escape debt if you can get a good paying job after college and assault the debt like mad but the odds are against you. The only debt I can see as being 'good' (in a double-edged sword way) is a mortgage, because if you ever happen to get into a hole at least you can sell it since you have the principle to repay the debt. If you do get a mortgage make sure it is fixed rate only (no adjustable rate ever). Follow this rule if you cannot afford it in cash, you cannot afford it- period. If there's something you want to buy but can't presently afford it, do it the old fashioned way- save for it!

If you are in debt, make every effort to get out now! The first step is to stop acculminating more debt. Stop using credit immediately, destroy your credit cards (cut them up, burn them, do whatever), and close your credit card accounts. Some 'experts' advise not to close your accounts as this lowers your credit score. I say close them and good riddens to them all, it's your call. If you can't bear to cut up your cards, freeze them in a bucket of water so you at least you won't have ready access to them. The next step is to pay off your balances from highest interest rate card first to the smallest; maybe you can refinance them too. Instead of paying monthly, pay bi-weekly so you'll save money on the interest. If you're in a real hole you will need professional help such as debt consolidation, negotiating a lump sum settlement, or as a last resort filling chapter 7 or 13 bankruptcy. Since these subjects are beyond the scope of this book I suggest seeking a professional finance adviser for more information about this.

Many people argue that to function to today's modern society you need to use credit cards. This is simply not true, even through I'm in my early 30's I have never applied for nor used a credit card. So how does one order on the internet, rent a car, buy airline tickets, or do other activities requiring a credit card. A logical alternative is to use a debit card. These draw on money you already have in an account. Which is good because it has a automatic failsafe against debt, no money in the account equals no purchase. Prepaid credit cards are also becoming available. Approval is instant with no credit check required. The money is drawn from a cash or money order deposit, bank account, or payroll. There is a initial setup fee and a reload fee when you deposit more money on it, but you're still saving money over regular credit cards because there is no interest rate.

If you decide at your peril that you must have a credit card 'in case of an emergency', make sure when you use the card it's for a REAL emergency (ordering a pizza and a case of beer at midnight don't count). Get a credit card with a low fixed interest rate, no annual fee, and no interest if you pay the balance in full. Then pay off the balance in full as soon as possible (within three months at the most, one month is even better) and always be on time.

Remember, in the privacy section I called banks the government's snitch and are best avoided. Here's another reason- outrageous fees such as overdraft penalties. If you don't believe me I suggest you read 'Your Bank is Ripping You Off' by Edward F. Mrkuicka, Jr. A good alternative to banks are credit unions, being that they are member owned and non-profit (everything a bank isn't) is reason enough to use one. You can find a good one close to you at www.creditunionsonline.com. Credit unions have in general lower minimum balances, free checking accounts, free overdraft protection, and lower service/ penalty fees. They also usually offer a higher interest on saving accounts and should you decide to make a deal with the devil a lower interest rate on loans. Another good alternate are Saving and Loans Associations which usually have lower service charges and minimum balances than banks.

Shelter

Rent whenever possible, I think home ownership is overrated. Some advantages of renting are freedom to move, no closing costs, no mortgage interest, no repair or upkeep bills, no homeowner's insurance, no property taxes, utilities sometimes are included, no yard maintenance costs, and the investment is small. Always rent houses over apartments because you usually get more room maybe even a backyard for your money. Try to rent from a person rather than a company because you are more likely to have some utilities paid plus they're less intrusive about privacy too. As far as landlords go the best type is one that's handicapped and lives in the next state. However, one that doesn't live near you is fine too. Aging landlords tend not to be as bad as young ones which tend to have a yuppie attitude. However, if you do decide to buy a home consider a fixer-upper. Do an inspection before buying and do most repairs yourself especially any cosmetic repairs like painting, carpeting, electricity, landscaping, or putting in new windows and doors. Avoid houses offered by realtors; they tend to be overpriced and pretentious.

You can try buying a home mortgage free using a land contract, here's how it works. Look for a house that's been on the market for years. Ask if you can buy the house on with down payment plus installments purchase contract. Agree on a sales price for the property with the terms providing a designated number of payments at predetermined intervals. The buyer receives the deed only after the seller receives most or all of the installment payments. Include a clause that allows the buyer to prepay the contract amount without penalties. Laws pertaining to this kind of agreement vary widely from state to state so be sure to review this contract with a real estate attorney before accepting the offer. They are couple of warnings about this kind of agreement. Check property records to make sure the title is clear (no mortgages, liens, or back taxes). If the title isn't and the seller doesn't take care of the costs still pending you could end of losing the property if you cannot pay these extra costs.

Some alternates to the own/ rent staple include getting a pickup camper; converting an old UPS truck, bread truck, or surplus school bus into a motor home. You would need access to bathing and cooking facilities. But this could be as simple as a stream and a cooking pit, cold water faucet and camping stove, or a local YMCA and a nearby microwave. Converting old yachts to a houseboat and hitching it to a dock is another possibility. One could buy a piece of remote, depleted land and put a trailer on it. You could even get free rent by becoming a property manager for an apartment building or a caretaker at a farm, resort off-season, or state/ national park. Look at www.caretaker.org website for more information. You could look into co housing communities on www.cohousing.org. Each person owns their own home but shares in the ownership of the common land and common house and sometimes a large garden. This can save costs as the community pools resources for a common goal such as bulk food, tools, repairs, etc.

If you're real bold or hard up squat an abandoned house or building. This can be difficult and is best done where they are very few or no neighbors nearby. You will need a propane camp stove, kerosene heater, water jugs, candles, and a plastic bucket for waste. Then seal the windows with plastic, seal the roof with tarpaper and plastic, and put wood over the holes in the floor. Some cities (though very few) have a law that if you can prove occupancy for 30 days (get mail delivered there) you are no longer a trespasser and thus must be evicted through the courts (this can take years). Additionally some cities have laws where you can claim "Adverse Possession", do the research for your locality. Try to get furniture and the utilities turned on so you won't look like crashers in case the police show up. You could try to find the owner and make a deal that you will watch over, clean, and fix up the house in exchange for free rent. Always keep receipts and take pictures as proof of repairs. The success of this really depends on location. If the house is in an unincorporated area, you will have no building code or permit bullshit to worry about.

Remember me saying not paying retail for anything, I meant it. Secondhand purchase furniture from garage sales, antique stores, auctions, clearance stores, or the thrift stores. Look for older and stronger pieces which have better workmanship not your modern particleboard piece of shit that'll fall apart in several years. Search curbsides for neighbor castoffs. Look on www.craigslist.com or www.freecycle.org for freebies. Sign up to clean dorm rooms at the end of the school year and you probably find lots of cool furnishings. You can build some furniture like bookcases and desks with some boards, cement blocks, wire spools, construction hardware, and some milk crates. Some creative people have made their own furniture from PVC pipes, fittings, pipe cement, a hacksaw, and tape measure. Check some of their creations at www.pvcplans.com. A desk can be made an old door, a 2x4 nailed to the wall, and a cabinet. Stain and varnish a flat piece of wood attach a painted stove base and viola, you have a coffee table. Painting, wallpapering, and putting up pictures are the cheapest ways to redecorate. Look for returned custom color paint at the store it's cheaper. You can shop carefully for or make fabrics for curtains and furniture throws. Get free carpet by visiting the carpet store dumpster just after closing or the curbside on trash night for rolls of carpet. If the carpet is very dirty, clean it with a spray carpet cleaner and wet it down with soapy ammonia water with a squeegee several times then rinse and air dry.

Always try to buy appliances secondhand as well from garage sales, outlet and clearance stores (most have only cosmetic damage such as a scratch or dent). Look into reconditioned appliances, auctions, and when relatives or neighbors upgrade or move as well. Buy this year's model at the end of the year. You may find good buys as stores try to sell off 'old' models to make room for new ones. Check around for floor models which could be brought at a reduced price, however insist on a new model full warranty first. Install and deliver (if you have the transportation) your own appliance rather than pay for it unless it's free. Never rent to own an appliance, you'll pay twice to five times the retail price of it. If you buy it at a thrift or garage sale- test it first, check cords and plugs, try the bulbs, and look in the battery compartment for corrosion. A nonfunctioning bargain is no bargain. Always check for quality and safety.

Most maintenance and repairs around the home need not be expensive either. You can save lots of money taking care of the basics unless it needs more brute strength than you have (find a friend). All you need is the knowledge and the tools. A basic toolset with a claw hammer, screwdrivers (flat and Phillips), pliers, wrenches (crescent, pipe, vice grips), and saws (hacksaw, circle or hardwood saw) will handle most projects that will arise. Just about most things can be fixed easily with wire, glue, duct tape, or booby pins. You can learn skills like sewing, welding, and refinishing on your own. Check trade schools for certain services, they're beauty schools that cut hair and automotive ones that fix cars. The students need practice under supervision and go there is a fraction of the cost than using a professional. If you know someone who likes to tinker around with cars, electronics, etc. you can pay them for minor repairs. If you are interesting in doing it the DIY way check out these handyman sites www.HGTV.com, www.DIYNetwork.com, www.homerepair.about.com, www.doityourself.com, www.ehow.com, and www.naturalhandyman.com. Also the books by Reader's Digest- New Fix-It-Yourself Manual and Complete Do-It-Yourself Manual or older Popular Mechanics and more recent Make and ReadyMade magazines make fine references.

Cleaning can be done on the cheap as well. All you need is baking soda, vinegar, ammonia, dish soap, and bleach. Baking soda is sort of like duct tape in many ways. It can be used as toothpowder, mouthwash, deodorant, athlete's foot powder, a pot scrubber, carpet deodorizer, facial scrub, battery acid neutralizer, or a fire extinguisher. A cloth soaked in a baking soda and water can be used to treat light burns, insect stings, and poison ivy. Use bleach for mainly disinfecting. Use one-quarter cup of white vinegar with a quart of water in a spray bottle to clean appliances, windows, mirrors, tile, and chrome. Using a quarter teaspoon of dish soap and one gallon of water you can wash dishes, mop floors, wash woodwork, clean stains, clean messy tools, and presoak greasy laundry. Use baking soda and water to a make a paste to scrub sinks, tubs, floors, and the stove. Use one half cup of ammonia mixed with one gallon of water to clean floors, walls, and the oven. As a drain cleaner- pour one-quarter cup of baking soda down the drain, followed with a half-cup of vinegar, let it fizz a bit, then flush down a gallon of boiling water. In addition, use old rags to clean instead of paper towels.

Food

Whenever possible you should buy your staples (bread, flour, grains, beans, canned goods, vegetables, dairy, sugar, salt, tea, coffee) in bulk and stick with generic brands. Most of the time the quality between brand name and generic is dubious, any benefit in buying brand name is mostly psychological. Buy food that's less than perfect such as day old bread, less than mint vegetables, or dented cans. Buy cheap food such as chicken, potatoes, flour, dry beans, dry milk, rice, pasta, macaroni and cheese, and ramen. Fruits and root vegetables such as apples, bananas, potatoes, onions, carrots, parsnips, turnips, beets, cabbage, tomatoes, collar and mustard greens are the cheapest. Avoid canned meat, pre-sliced cold cuts, junk food (cookies and chips), prepackaged food, frozen food like pizzas and TV dinners as their cost outstrips any quantity and quality they may have. If you must buy junk food snacks buy them in large containers and on sale. Better yet, learn to make your own snacks. They are cookbooks that have recipes for donuts, potato chips, beef jerky, tortilla chips, onion rings, applesauce, or pudding which can be made for pennies on the dollar. Try to buy frozen vegetables rather than canned which are less nutritious. Only buy cheap cuts of meat (hamburger, pork steak or roast, frozen chicken quarters, roast hens) and on sale (never over $2.50/ lb.). Certain holidays of the year are best to buy meat on sale (corned beef before St. Patrick's Day, hot dogs before Fourth of July, Turkey before Thanksgiving, or Ham before Christmas and Easter). Sales are a good time to stock up too, if you can buy twice as much as usual. To be truly frugal you could buy just wheat flour, brown rice, butter, olive oil, and nuts then hit a natural food dumpster and easily just spend $50-$100 a month.

Avoid impulse buying, make a shopping list and stick to it. Never shop when you are hungry (or stoned for that matter). If you do you WILL buy on impulse (trust me). Experiment with and substitute cheaper alternatives, for example buy oatmeal instead of cornflakes, dry milk instead of whole milk, dry beans instead canned beans, block cheese instead of grated cheese, turkey instead of chicken, or egg noodles instead of macaroni. Avoid sodas and drink water, tea, kool aid, or lemonade instead. Avoid readymade baked goods; make your own cakes and cookies instead. In the aisles, look high and look low as the most expensive items are placed at eye level. Leave the credit card and checks at home, shop with cash only and you'll be less likely to overspend. Don't rush your shopping- take time to read the labels, check the cost per serving, and compare brands. Because of rising oil and food costs some packaging is being downsized (instead of 16 oz. it's now 15 oz.)- watch out for this! Never buy non-food items (like toilet paper) at the supermarket, they are cheaper elsewhere. Use cloth towels and napkins instead of the paper products or loot napkins from restaurants. Shop alone, other people will 'help' fill your shopping cart (especially children). Don't shop at the first of the month or right before the holidays, some supermarkets raise prices then. Take advantage of coupons and rebates for items you want to buy only. Use discount cards if they have them (but under an alternate name, go back to the privacy section for more on this). Buy seasonally (no watermelon in January or apples in July). Buy regionally too (no lobster in Colorado and no beef in New York), limit these foods since you have to pay for the shipping to get it there.

Learn how to make your own homemade salads, bread, and soups. Plus soup is cheap and filling food. You can find recipes for these at www.recipesource.com/misc/mixes. When meat is called for in a recipe; fill it in with vegetables, beans, and pasta instead. Stretch meatloaf and hamburger by adding breadcrumbs, crushed crackers, rice, or oatmeal. Try eating less meat or cheese and more fish like canned mackerel, herring, salmon, sardines, or tuna. Eggs, peanut butter, dried beans, peas, lentils, oatmeal, skim milk are cheaper protein sources than meat too. If you buy meat, buy it in bulk from farmer's markets in the city or farmers in the country. You could become a part time vegetarian eating several meatless meals a week. If you have the discipline, consider stopping to eat meat altogether (your wallet and heart will thank you). If you have a limited schedule to cook, use your freezer by preparing several meals weekly then freeze them and heat up portions as needed- it's cheaper and healthier than TV dinners. Experiment with spices and find out the best mix for your palate. I myself am a freak for garlic, curry, and olive oil. Whatever you do, don't waste food or throw anything away (in many less affluent countries this is considered an insult). There's no such thing as leftovers, if you don't eat it and it's not spoiled then freeze and use it for the next meal. Save everything even the broth from boiling that chicken, freeze it and use it in future recipes.

Forgo the regular supermarket and use warehouse club stores instead. They have the best buys for bulk foods. You can find fifty pound bags of flour and rice, five pound bags of pasta, ten pound packs of ground beef, quart boxes of dry milk, five pound blocks of cheese, or gallon jars of condiments. They also stock many times #10 (restaurant size) cans of instant potatoes, canned vegetables, beans, and chili. Natural food co-ops and farmers markets are good for bulk fruits, vegetables, and grain (plus many times they're organic too). Discount bread stores many times have fresh bread, rolls, hamburger and hot dog buns, baked goods, and snacks at reduced prices. Buy a bunch and freeze them for a rainy day. Bagel shops sell at 50% discount an hour before closing. El cheapo (my word) supermarkets such as Save A Lot and Aldi have excellent deals as well. If you're looking for something a little different try some the ethnic markets in your areas. If you want really cheap go to a livestock feed store and buy 100 lb. sacks of whole wheat, yellow corn, and oats. Just be sure it's not treated grain and you will need a grinder to process it. Learn how to preserve your food by canning, dehydrating, pickling, and making jams.

Consider growing your own food by planting a garden, fruit tree, or berry patch. If you can find a spot that gets sun 6-8 hours a day, close to home and water (soil and climate permitting) you can start one. If your neighborhood has a community garden you can start there. If you have very little room check out this site www.squarefootgardening.com for some ideas. Try growing hi-yield plants like tomatoes, beans, peas, lettuce, squash, cabbage, spinach, onions, garlic, peppers, cucumbers, or zucchini. Start from seed in egg cartons, yogurt and butter tubs then transplant those to the garden. Make it all organic with no commercial fertilizer, just make your compost and mulch the garden. You can start a compost pile by making walls from recycled 2x4's and chicken wire then put in grass clippings, leaves, wood chips, coffee grinds, shredded newspaper, egg shells, kitchen and veggie scraps, hair, or other decaying matter in the mix. Some landfills give away free mulch too. You could also raise livestock such as rabbits or chickens. With rabbits all you need is a hutch, dry bedding, food, water, a couple of dows, and one buck. With chickens you need just a couple boxes and an enclosed space for one rooster and a couple setting hens. If you have the land and time you could raise ducks, guinea fowl, or goats.

Get your food for free if you're in the country by killing it (hunting or fishing) or in the city by foraging for it (dumpsters, food banks, feedings, or government surplus). Sometimes you can ask the grocery store for fresh vegetable trimmings. Ask for unsold produce from the farmer's market at sundown. Hari Krishna temples on Sundays and Sikh temples once or twice a week have free dinners. Many times supermarket samples, store openings, club meetings, and frat parties have free chow. Look for any event that mentions 'refreshments will be served.' If you have a wide network of friends, relatives, or workmates you can mooch some meals once in a while. Never turn down a free meal. If you don't want it, save it for later or give it to someone else needier than you are. Search the internet for companies offering free samples, coupons, and deals at sites like www.keycodes.com, www.currentcodes.com, www.afullcup.com, www.dealcatcher.com, www.couponmom.com, www.retalmenot.com, www.redplum.com, www.fatwallet.com, www.freebies4mom.com, and. Google under "blog giveaways" too, you may never what you may win. In you're in the country, after a harvest you may be able to with the owner's permission glean their farm fields and pick up whatever is left over. Study wild plants by getting some good field guides (a good one to start with would be "Field Guide to Edible Wild Plants" by Bradford Angier) and adding a little to your diet at a time condition your system to them. Dandelions are a good one to start with since they're easy to spot and the whole plant is edible. But be sure you know what you're picking, if you don't the plant may make you ill or even kill you.

If you're really desperate or just a kleptomaniac you could shoplift your food. You'll need a loose open jacket with big inside pockets. Using a shopping cart, roam the aisles putting toilet paper and other bulky items in the deep part of the cart. Place the food you want to steal in the baby seat part. At the right time; like in an aisle with no mirrors, cameras, or witnesses slide the food in your inside pockets. Try to remove packaging and unwrapping meat or cheese before sliding the food. Also fresh vegetables, fruits, and frozen food are usably the safest to snatch. Another unorthodox tactic is gypsy scrounging- dress up neat and clean, hit a big hotel, go to the banquet room, and pig out on the grub while 'mingling' with the guests. After the party, ask a waiter for leftovers to take to 'your room'. Finally, if there's an art galley opening in town- crash it and gouge yourself on the cheese, crackers, appetizers, and wine.

When going out be careful, very careful!! You want to eat food and drink beverages not money! In the movies a $2.50 soda would have cost 50 cents in the supermarket. A $3.50 mixed drink in a bar is made from one $10 bottle of booze. One restaurant dinner is worth one week of groceries. Vending machines are a big rip off. Likewise, bottled water is maybe the biggest rip off of all, which costs 200 to 1,000% more than tap water. Some restaurants have gone as far as refusing to serve tap water forcing you to buy it instead. Never buy bottled water ever unless the tap water is really bad or contaminated. If the tap water is really that horrible get a Brita filter instead. When going to work or traveling pack your own lunch and eat a good breakfast at home so you can avoid the takeout at restaurants and rest stop cafeterias (which are grossly overpriced). Carry water with you when you go out so you won't be tempted to use the vending machines. Make your own 'take out' style meals like pizza, Mexican or Asian foods. Consider organizing a potluck with some friends or have a picnic in the park instead of eating out. Look for events that entertain and feed you at the same time. If there is a culinary school in your area check if they have an onsite restaurant. It is usually cheaper to eat out at them. Cafes tend to be cheaper too. Try dining at church, American Legion, Elk Lodge, and other fundraisers. Order only from the dollar menu and avoid the soft drinks at fast food restaurants. If you must have one, check and see if their soda machine is self serve. If it is, ask only for a cup of water (if you're lucky you won't even have to pay for the cup) and then dump the water and help yourself to some soda. Pilfer a bunch of ketchup, mustard, and salt packets too while you're at it! If you do eat out at a restaurant- eat for lunch or breakfast (many times the same items are half price) or the cheapest side dish instead of dinner, check to see if they have a 'reduced rate' on certain days and hours or for seniors or children, and drink only water with a lemon then use the sugar packets to make lemonade. Other eating out strategies include looking for coupons before going, looking for the daily specials, splitting an order with someone else, going for lunch buffets, skipping the drinks and desserts, and avoiding tourist or high profile restaurants. Some restaurants have birthday clubs offering free meals on your birthday you can sign up for. When you finish eating, always ask for a doggie bag and take home everything not eaten (why throw out food you paid for).

Clothing

I personally spend next to nothing on clothes except for an occasional visit to the thrift store. You don't need to have expensive clothes or even a lot of them. I have only half a dresser full of clothes and still can find employment, go to parties, and even have a girlfriend. You probably have a closet full of clothes you never wear. It may still have the price tag attached! If it does, sell it at consignment shop like Buffalo Exchange and pocket the money. The fewer clothes you have, the more you'll save on laundry too! Wear darker colors too, as this saves on laundry since you won’t have to do a wash as often. With the exception of socks, underwear, and sometimes footwear always buy clothing secondhand (Salvation Army, Goodwill, flea markets, yard sales in affluent neighborhoods, or eBay). If this is too expensive hit up the free box and clothes closets. Also always search the pockets of clothes when shopping used, you may find money. Buy mostly work clothes as they are the most durable. Also for the best deals buy clothing off season and look for items with slight cosmetic defects or irregularities. When buying check the pockets (you may find money), zippers, buttons, and for rips and holes. Slight damage may be able to be repaired- it's your call. Wear it till it's worn out, repair don't throw out torn or worn clothing. Sew up minor rips and holes. Cut worn long sleeves to make short sleeve shirts. Make patches from worn leather clothes and luxury car seats (like Cadillacs). If it's really old- make a quilt, a rug, or cut them up for rags. Care for boots by rubbing in Neat's foot oil and rain wear by spraying on silicone waterproofing. Avoid spending money on luxury clothing unless you occupation requires it. If you need a cheap suit buy a sports jacket, a turtleneck, and some work pants at the thrift store. Buy clothing that doesn't need dry cleaning (those bills can cost you a bundle). Army surplus clothing such as fatigues, ponchos, combat boots, jeans, sweatshirts, t-shirts, and field jackets are good buys. For cold weather just get a wool shirt, wool pants, ski cap, gloves, and a parka, it's all you'll need for most climates. If you volunteer at a thrift shop warehouse you get first pickings of the discards. You can find good discards dumpster diving in upper class neighborhoods too. Cheap bedding can be made from army blankets and sleeping bags. If you are talented enough you can buy fabric and a secondhand sewing machine and make your own clothing. If you wish to try hand dyeing clothes in the washing machine check out this site www.pburch.net/dyeing.shtml.

Utilities

Utilities are one expense that can be managed with common sense and paying attention to your consumption. First of all, keep the lights off in the daytime unless necessary- use sunlight. Turn off all lights, appliances, TV, stereo, or anything that doesn't have to be on when not in use. Use a nightlight in the bathroom and keep a flashlight next to the bed at night. Use manual appliances like can openers and knives instead of electric ones. Replace incandescent bulbs with compact fluorescent ones of the lowest wattage possible as they consume less energy for the same light output. Turn off your computer monitor and videogames when not in use. When not using the computer during the day use an energy saving setting like hibernate mode. At night turn it off with the power strip switch. Unplug electronics and unused appliances at night to prevent 'phantom loads'. Buy energy efficient appliances (especially refrigerators and washers). Refrigerators are big energy users, if you live alone get a smaller fridge. Keep the refrigerator coils clean and don't overload the refrigerators with food. On the contrary keep the freezer as full as possible. If you don't have enough to fill it, use bottles of water. If your oven is electric use the toaster, crock-pot, or microwave over the regular oven as it uses less power. If you use the 'interior' of the oven (not the burner) multitask and make several dishes at once. Also turn off burners and oven a few minutes before food is done; the heat already present will cook the food. Lower the temperature on the water heater to the lowest you can live with (120 degrees is good), then insulate it too. Wash clothes in cold water and only in full loads. Air dry clothes or dry over heater vents whenever possible as dryers use a lot of juice. Store batteries for portable electronics in the refrigerator, they will last longer or use rechargeable Ni-Cad batteries.

The highest use of water in a household is the toilet, bathing, laundry, dishwashing, and cooking. Consumption from actually drinking it is a distant last so usage here can be trimmed as well. Cut down on showers and baths, use sponge baths more often. Use low-flow showerheads and install aerators in bathroom faucet. Don't run the tap continuously when shaving or brushing your teeth. Put a container filled with a half gallon of water in the toilet tank. Do not flush the toilet unnecessarily by using it as a trash disposal and flush only after it's been used 2-3 times. Wash only full loads and limit permanent press cycles which use a third more water. If you have a very small load, hand wash and rinse it in the sink. Buy clothes and household items that don't have to be washed separately so you'll do fewer loads. Heat a kettle of water rather running hot water from the tap. Use water from boiling eggs or pasta to water plants. Repair dripping faucets as these can waste 350 gallons of water a month! Turn off faucets immediately after each use. If it isn't urgent that the car gets washed, let the rain do it- rainwater is free.

To save heating energy costs the magic word is to insulate. Cover the windows with plastic sheeting, bubble wrap, blankets, heavy curtains, or Styrofoam or rubber slabs cut to fit them. Seal air leaks around doorways and window frames with caulk or foam. Fix cracks and holes in the wall with plaster or spackling. Don't forget about plumbing, wiring, and light fixtures which penetrate into the attic or crawl space either. Place stoppers under all doors to keep out drafts. This can be a pillowcase stuffed with newspaper, rags, sand or a rolled up rug or towel. Newspaper can be your best friend. Put a layer of 5-6 pages under the rug, staple a layer of the same on the walls and cover with a sheet, and place another layer under the mattress. If you can afford it install storm doors and windows then install thermal shades. Seal and insulate heating ducts as well as the attic. Wrap and tape layers of newspaper around hot water pipes.

Tape the dryer vent closed with foam tape. Insulate yourself too, wear layers (sweater and long johns), wear socks and slippers, wear a hat, use more blankets or two liter hot water bottles, and eat or drink warm foods (soup, stew, chili, warm bread, tea, or cocoa). Take advantage of any heat produced (hot bathwater, candles, oil lamps, even guests (their body heat warms the room!). Make sure furniture is not blocking the heating vents. Clean regularly the filter of the heating unit you're using and dust radiator surfaces, dust impedes heat flow. Instead of an electric heating pad pour a bunch of rice in fabric sack then heat it the microwave a couple of minutes and sleep on that. Close doors and heating vents to any rooms not in use. Then you can lower the thermostat at night. After using the oven, turn it off and open the door to help heat the room. Turn off the furnace and use an electric hot oil radiator taking it in the room with you. That way you heat only one room instead of the entire house.

You could consider heating with wood instead depending on the area you live in, the more rural the better. It has the advantages of being a renewable resource and it isn't subject to power outages. Depending upon availibity wood can cost \$50-\$100 a cord. However, if you look carefully you can find many free sources of fuel such as pallets, tree trimmings from the neighbors, from landfills, slabs trimmed from logs at mills, swapping with the firewood supplier, scavenging fallen trees and discarded fence posts, or even rolling newspapers and cardboard into logs. If you don't have a fireplace a wood stove can made from a 55 gallon drum and a stovepipe. Wood needs to season at least six months before using. Do not use greenwood, as this has creosote and can cause a chimney fire. If your wood is scavenged make sure it hasn't been treated. Softwoods like Pine and Cotton wood burns quick and hot, while hardwoods such as Oak, Cherry, Apple, and Black Walnut burns slow and hot. It is best to use a combination of these two for a good fire.

You can stay cool too and save energy costs. Cover the windows with blinds and shades to keep out the heat from the sun in the day and open the windows at night. Use an outdoor grill instead the stove. Unless you are elderly or in poor health do without an air conditioner and use ceiling fans instead. Use exhaust fans in the kitchen and bathroom. You can make a evaporative air cooler which is a big fan with a wet burlap cloth in front of it. Hose down the entire house with water; it will chill the air that moves in the house. Do stuff in the basement; it's usually ten degrees cooler than the rest of the house. Keep anything that produces heat (including lights) off.

Try to get a flat rate phone service with local service only. Don't pay for nonessentials and extras you won't use. Only use operator assistance in an emergency, rates for these services are high. Use a free 411 service number instead paying. Call long distance off-peak or block it altogether and use only prepaid phone cards, dial around numbers, and cellphones. Drop the landline and use a cellphone only or just use e-mail and write letters more. If you use the postal system a lot reuse the envelopes and reuse the stamps by soaking them in rubbing alcohol to remove postmarks then glue them on the envelope being used. If you have a computer and broadband internet you can use VoIP phone services like skype.com, vonage.com, gizmo5.com, voice.yahoo.com, or majicjack.com which allows you to make free long distance calls to other subscribers or very cheap (2 cents a minutes) to non-subscribers from your computer. VoIP may have privacy benefits over landline as well; I don't know much on this but check out www.zfoneproject.com for more information. If you want an extra phone line go to Radio Shack get 50 feet of phone wire, a phone jack and do your own installation. There is a $10 a month DSL service available that AT&T is very supersecret about but it's only available in 22 states. Check the internet to see if you live in one of those states. I prefer to do without cable or satellite TV being that it's interesting to think most people lived without these as little as twenty years ago. If you must have cable TV stick with the basic package without the movie and premium channels.

Now if you're real hardcore you could consider living off the grid altogether. Your light can be from a kerosene, propane, or dual fuel Coleman lantern. Heating and cooking could be done by kerosene, propane, or wood heaters and stoves. Because of the fumes they can put off always have adequate ventilation when using these. To produce electricity use photovoltaic solar panels or a 3-8 HP small gas engine (like on a lawnmower) and a car alternator connected to a 12 volt deep cycle RV battery. There are many 12 volt appliances available at www.jcwhitney.com. If you want to run AC equipment you will need an inverter. This drains the juice from the battery faster too. I would use two batteries- use one while the other is charging. This entire system could set up for $300-$400 (cheaper with used parts). Avoid the gasoline AC generators as they are expensive to operate and require too much maintenance. Rainwater can be collected with a clean roof, gutter system, and a holding tank. For waste disposal a self-made or manufactured composting toilet can be used. A good source for off the grid equipment is www.lehmans.com (it's like a Sears for the Amish).

Health Care

The best way to save on health care is to prevent yourself from needing it in the first place. Practice preventive care and self-care. This is a no brainer but I'll say it anyway- get proper nutrition, drink lots of water, exercise regularly, get adequate rest, watch your weight, think about safety around you to prevent injuries, reduce stress, and limit high risk activities. At the risk of sounding like a hypocrite, stop or try to stop smoking. Try to eliminate or limit unhealthy food (refined sugar, white bread, soft drinks, junk food, high fats, red meat) in your diet. One good way to do this is to stop buying it at the grocery altogether. Reduce your calorie intake by eating a big breakfast (it's the most important meal) and eating smaller portions during the day. Eat less- most Americans eat too much anyway. Also start taking multivitamins daily. Avoid over the counter drugs like laxatives and sleep aids. Eat a proper diet and get proper sleep and you won't need them. You don't need an expensive health club membership to get exercise. You can get lots of exercise for cheap at the YMCA or free by yourself- walking, jogging, biking, hiking, dancing, playing basketball or tennis, or take the stairs instead of the escalator or elevator. You can make cheap weights with one pound cans of food or plastic jugs of water. If you find or already have a physical intensive job (construction or farm work) you get a workout with pay.

Avoid the emergency room except for a real emergency like a heart attack, major trauma, shock to allergens or poisons, or uncontrollable bleeding as they are very expensive. If you have to go to the ER use a car instead of the ambulance if possible. Don't spend money on medical exams every year unless you have chronic medical problems. If you donate plasma you will receive a free mini physical; get checked for HIV, TB, and Hepatitis plus they financially compensate you. Get medical procedures or treatment outside the hospital, it's cheaper. Look for free screenings for blood pressure, dental, diabetes, bone density, fitness, hearing, vision, and immunizations. Look into medical or dental schools, they may offer treatment or tests for less because they need guinea pigs. Community health services are cheaper than private doctors too. If anyone in your family is a military veteran check VA hospitals and clinics, you may get a discount. Most health departments and social services will refer for free or low cost medical exams, immunization, well-baby care, prenatal care, mental counseling. Healthcare workers may be able to get discounts at their hospital too. Some dentists will let you paint their house, clean their gardens, or babysit for a trade; leave a letter at their office. Use home testing kits for things like pregnancy or glaucoma instead of going to the doctor. Buy generic prescriptions and vitamins. Look in doctor magazines for free samples of drugs and order them or ask your doctor for them. You could try getting medicine across the border in Mexico and save up to 50-80%. At www.pharagroup.com you can order imported prescriptions on the cheap. I've also heard of people finding near equivalents of their medicine from veterinarians again for less. Major pharmaceutical companies have programs for people who qualify for free prescriptions. Contact them and ask for a form to fill out with a doctor. Learn first aid, CPR, and stock a first aid kit at home to treat minor problems and deal with serious emergencies until a doctor can be found. Don't over sanitize your home with anti-bacterial products; it makes it harder for your immune system to build up. Always get a second opinion for expensive medical treatment. Examine any medical bill and look for errors like duplicate testing, it happens more than you think. Consider alternative medicine such as herbalism, acupuncture, and homeopathy. A good resource for this is www.naturalhealthweb.com. If you're under 40 with no serious high risk factors in your family history, no hazardous work, and in good health you could get by with little or no insurance at all. Research state health insurance plans for low income families. Simple Care (www.simplecare.com) provides an alternative health care service to its members. For $20 per year you go to a member list of providers and get large discounts (up to 30-50%) off their regular rates. Good websites for additional information on health care include www.doctoryourself.com, www.medicinenet.com, www.mayoclinic.com, and www.healthy.net.

Personal care can be done on the cheap as well. Stop haircuts and hair care at the barber shop and beauty salon. Cut, shampoo, dye, color, set, or perm your own hair. If the job is really complicated, call the local cosmetology or barber school for an appointment and information when students will do it but under an instructor's observation. Also occasionally you can be a model for instructors that demonstrate haircutting, conditioning, styling, and other procedures to students at local schools. Never throw out soap, squeeze the moist pieces together to make one big piece. Stretch liquid products out too by diluting them with water. Get the last bit of contents of shampoo, liquid soap, etc. by storing upside down so everything drains down for use. Use rubbing alcohol or baking soda instead of deodorant. Instead of mouthwash, gargle with a cup of four parts water and one part salt. Use cheap hair conditioner or olive oil in lieu of shaving cream. Another way is to make your own shaving soap by melting dove soap in a double boiler, adding one tablespoon of avocado olive oil, and letting cool before using. A body wash can be made with sea salt and baby oil. Last but not least, food banks and drop in centers sometimes have trail sizes of beauty products in small buckets.

Transportation

Always buy simple used cars (like old V8's and Japanese cars) besides being cheaper in terms of maintenance, insurance, tax, and registration they're also less likely to be broken into, stolen, or carjacked. Buy for practicality not ego. Look in the classified ads first to avoid used car lots as the salesmen are sharks. Sometimes rental car companies, auctions, dealer repo sales, and surplus police cruisers can yield good bargains. Also asking friends, neighbors, or co-workers first can steer you to good deals. When buying a car whenever possible pay for a used car in full to avoid car payments. Check consumer reports and get a car with a high safety rating which will cost you less insurance. When you find a potential car to buy view the car's story online at www.carfax.com or www.autocheck.com which will tell you about any previous accidents (if any) and previous owners. Ask the seller questions about mileage, tires, condition, motor work needed, does the car overheat, motor ever been replacing, been in accident, what parts are new on it, or does car smoke. This may seem like a lot of questions but an honest seller shouldn't mind. Before buying a car from anyone have it checked by a mechanic before signing the title. Always try to test drive the car before buying; noting if it goes uphill easily, overheats easily, or if it has any 'off sounds'. Unfortunately, with street buys they have been scams involving stolen cars lately. Therefore, it's advisable to get the seller's name, address, and license plate number then run the plate and check if the registration is still current before going to his home for the car. When buying, check the seller's ID to see if the papers of the car match. But do NOT give the seller your name and address. You do not want a paper trail, it is possible to be frugal and maintain privacy too.

There are some tricks to save on insurance as well (Warning- these are ALL very illegal). One can simply register the car in an area where insurance rates are cheaper than where you normally reside. For example, you register the car in rural Pennsylvania when you actually live in Brooklyn, NY. Since the insurance company thinks you "live" in Amish country instead of "Crooklyn" you get a cheaper premium. You could avoid insurance altogether by scanning someone else's insurance card on a computer, substitute your name for theirs, put in an imaginary insurer's name, and print it on card stock paper. Then stick this in an official looking envelope and carry this in the glove compartment. Needless to say if you employ any of these tricks drive extra safe and do NOT have an accident!

To save on gas, use your car to travel to work only, run errands weekly, and use the most direct route. Use a discount card to buy gas. Fill up when the tank is half empty. Search www.gasbuddy.com and www.gaspricewatch.com to find the cheapest price on gas. Coast when possible and turn off the car at stop lights. Keep your tires inflated to their correct pressure.

Following preventative maintenance schedules indicated in

the owner's manual will help keep your car out the shop and money in your pocket. Most routine maintenance such as replacing the air/ oil filter and wiper blades, cleaning the spark plugs, refilling the oil and fluids, and checking brake pads can be done yourself. If you must have repairs done see if you can find a reputable home based mechanic first. Since he/ she doesn't have to pay rent on a shop the price will be cheaper and 'off the books'. Don't use the car wash, wash your own car. Get a Chilton repair book for your model or the book 'Auto Repair for Dummies' and a tool set with open end and socket wrenches, screwdrivers, pliers, files, grips, and gauges. If you have the time, take an auto repair class at a local community college.

To reduce wear, tear, and save gas use your car only for long distance trips, bike or use public transportation in the city. You could consider renting a car only for trips and moves and skip owning a car altogether. If you don't live in the country it may be a good option to not have a car at all. Think of all the money you'll save on registration, insurance, gas, maintenance, parking fees, and traffic tickets. You can buy a bike for less cost than putting new tires on a car. Plus they are easier and cheaper to fix than a car. If you don't like peddling you could alternately get a used 125cc moped and since they get around 100mpg you'll still be saving a ton of gas money. Most medium to large cities (with the exception of Los Angeles) have excellent public transportation systems. I have never had a car in my life and the only time I had a problem was living in northern rural New Mexico (lucky I was able to hitch most places there). Most bus lines, subways, and commuter trains have a monthly pass you can buy to get the most for your money. A best case scenario (although not always possible) would be living in walking distance to work, school, supermarket, library, and the park. If your destination is close enough just hop on a bike or walk there, you'll save money (and aggravation) on gas and parking plus get some exercise.

Entertainment

While not considered a necessity people expend insane amounts of money in this area. First, don't buy a new TV, stereo, VCR, or DVD- buy it used. Don't buy new DVD's either. Record good programs from public TV or borrow them at the library. Instead of going to the movie theater; buy used or rent movies, use the $1 redbox kiosks, watch them on TV and on Youtube.com, or download from P2P networks. If you must go see that picture on the big screen find one where a worker can get you in for free, you can sneak into, or go to a cheap matinee night (and bring your own popcorn and candy too). Reduce attending expensive entertainment such as plays, theater, opera, concerts, and cabarets. Volunteering as an usher or ticket taker at cultural performance houses is good way to see these theaters, musicals, or symphonies for free. You can also find out when intermission hits, join the crowd returning but just try being the last ones in to find the empty unsold seats. Find when TV shows with live audiences have free tickets. Check out more zoos, botanical gardens, museums, art galleries, planetariums, and state parks which usually if not free are cheaper than the movies and probably better for the mind as well. These places usually have special discounts for students, seniors, children, the disabled, families, and groups; ask if you don't know. If you like beer or wine, take a tour of the local brewery or winery- you get free samples too. Alternatively, I hear one could buy movie tickets in bulk at AAA and Costco. If you live near a college campus sometimes they may be theater productions, guest speakers, poetry readings, film screenings, art openings, museum tours, and sports events happening there (sometimes with free food too). Look around in the newspaper or Craigslist.com for lectures, demonstrations, training workshops offered by various organizations, clubs, groups, government agencies, and businesses.

Remember what I said about never buying retail that includes music too in spades! Buy your CD's used from bargain music stores, burn your own CD's, tape music off the college stations or your friends tapes, peer to peer file share MP3's, tape trade, scam the BMG music club for free CD's (then rip the tracks and sell the CD's), shoplift CD's, buy used tapes and records at thrift stores, anything but DO NOT buy your music retail ever!! I would make an exception for underground and DIY artists but don't even think of giving the mainstream corporations your money. Why does it cost $20 retail to buy music put on a 50 cent CD?? That scam is almost as bad as the bottled water. Thinking about it why buy music so much anyway get a guitar, banjo, keyboard, flute, harmonica, some scrap metal, or whatever gather some friends and make your own music.

Try to take up an inexpensive hobby like hiking, camping, karaoke, baking, card games, chess, circus acts (like juggling or magic tricks), creative writing, drawing, painting, collage, silk screening, sewing, knitting, stencils, puppets, wheat pasting, building bikes, target shooting, athletics at YMCA or local park, making jewelry, candle making, screen-printing, or urban exploration. You could try your hand at self-publishing books (like this one) or zines. Instead buying of shelling out $300 for a Weii, play some classic video games off a used Sega, Nintendo 64, or Playstation 1. I've seen used consoles for as cheap as $30. You could get a cheap digital video camera with a 1 gigabyte SD card start filming then edit it on library computer and share it with friends online. Another cheap hobby to try is radio monitoring with an inexpensive shortwave radio or a police scanner. Many times you will know about what's happening before it's on the news (and sanitized by them too!). Engage in nothing expensive like boating, skiing, diving, or golf.

One good hobby to try is home brewing, it is fun and saves drinking money. It need not be expensive as long as you don't buy one of those expensive beer making kits. Although, home brewing purists will cringe at this- all you need really is some gallon jugs and large balloons. One favorite and easy recipe of mine is homemade cider which requires only 1 gallon pasteurized apple cider, 1 cup of brown sugar, 1 packet of yeast, and a dash of cinnamon and nutmeg. First clean out the gallon jug with bleach, pour all the ingredients in, cover the mouth with a balloon, wait 1-2 weeks, refrigerate, and drink. Since when the yeast is active it will fill the balloon with carbon dioxide which must be let out when full, so you must check the jug now and then or it may explode leaving quite a mess. Also be careful not to let any air inside the jug as this may spoil the cider. While brewing beer is cheaper than buying, the opposite is true for liquor plus you have to worry about safety. The cheapest liquor out the store is vodka. If you smoke consider stopping. If you're like me and can't kick yet then buy loose tobacco and roll your own. If you're not used to it may take practice but it's cheaper, plus since they're stronger you'll smoke less, and they have less additives making them slightly less hazardous. At specialty tobacco shops you can find rolling tobacco as low as $15 for a one pound bag!

Go to more parties (ones with free food or booze are of course the best but potlucks, BYOB, or buy a cup keggers are cool too) instead of clubs and bars, you'll probably meet better people there too. Invite some friends over, pool your money for drinks and movies then have a movie night. If you must go to a bar, buy some beer at the liquor store first and sneak it in the bar, then buy a pitcher after drinking it fill it with the beer you snook in. Like sports, instead of going to the pro games go to college or high school games. Like to shop, go thrift shop and garage sale hopping. In the summer check out free concerts, plays, special festivals, or other live acts in the local park. If you go to the zoo or amusement park a lot, see about getting a season pass. Go to book superstores like Borders, Barnes and Noble but DON"T buy anything just grab a book sit down and you can read for hours (I've even taken notes before, just don't be obvious). Stop all newspaper and magazine subscriptions- scam them by filling out those cards under a bogus name, checking the bill me later box, and mailing it. You can read them at the library, on the internet, or search in the trash after the morning for old newspapers. If you gamble (playing lotto (aka-stupidity tax), numbers, craps, racetrack, poker, blackjack, whatever) STOP now- gambling and frugality don't mix. If you have an expensive addiction, pull yourself out of it or trade it for a cheaper one. Depending on your creed consider firing the Christmas holidays. Since I don't celebrate it really I save a lot from not spending it on gifts. I don't give any gifts nor do I expect any. If you do celebrate it shop for Christmas gifts year round to get the sales and make your own Christmas cards. While not my style I heard going to country type outings like local dinners, fairs, rodeos, square dances, and auto racing are economical.

Dumpster Diving

The willingness to sift through the excess waste of society is what separates the casual frugal person from the hardcore frugal one. They say that one person trash is another treasure. You'd be surprised of all the treasure I been finding for over 15 years in those smelly dumpsters. A short list of finds include food, furniture, stereos, clothes, boots, gourmet food, tapes, records, construction supplies, appliances, lamps, books, computers, tools, pornography, videos, CD's, information, even liquor. Some people have been known to find working computers, old school video games, televisions, power tools, bicycles, video games, drugs, money, firearms, and corpses too (just kidding!); however I haven't been that fortunate yet. To get started you first need to learn the trash disposal and pickup schedule. Commercial places are usually daily while residential are weekly. You should dress in old and tough clothes like work boots, jeans, flannel, and leather gloves. Useful gear to take along include a flashlight (illuminate dark spots), knife (opening trash bags), handkerchief (in case you spill something messy on you), and a backpack (for carrying the goods you find). Though I never used one- some people use a dive stick, a pole with a hook on the end for reaching trash bags far in the dumpster. Other optional items are a bicycle or car (so you can cover more territory) and a milk crate (as a stool for tall dumpsters). If you will be driving take a yellow pages along. So if you think of a type of business to dive, you can look it up, and drive there. The best time overall to dive is early evenings, it'll be dark enough to not attract too much attention but not late enough as to arouse suspicion In addition, some seasons are better for certain diving. The best for food is the fall and winter because food less likely to spoil. But the best for college areas is mid-May/ June, last August, and mid-December because of semester changes.

Now you're probably wondering where do you go for all the good stuff. Good spots for food include Dunkin Donuts, Brueggar Bagels, bakeries (bread, baked goods, out of date pastry), supermarkets for produce, 7-11 type convenience stores (expired sandwiches and dairy), and pizzerias like Dominios and Pizza Hut (extra pizzas not delivered). Co-ops and natural grocery stores are great because the food is better and since they're anti-consumerist identify with divers. If you doubt the edibility of anything, let your nose be your judge. If don't smell or look right, toss it. Avoid dairy, meat, and salads in the summer. Stay away from actual restaurant dumpsters; they're quite disgusting because they throw out all the food together. A better way is to befriend a busboy or server and ask for food five minutes before closing. This is good at some fast food places and food courts in malls too. Just don't overdo these.

For other goodies check out florists, thrift stores, strip malls, department stores, bookstores, motels, hotels, toy stores, electronic stores, craft stores, bicycle shops, carpet outlets, demolition/ construction sites, furniture stores, garden stores, drug stores, video rentals, computer repair shops, cell phone and satellite TV shops, military surplus stores, and plant nurseries. When you start out you'll end up with a grab bag of stuff which may or may not useful to you. For example, plant nurseries usually toss lots of plants and dirt which I don't have much use for but if you're into gardening that's a different story. Watch for when residents are moving out houses and apartments, college campuses are vacating their dorms, and businesses are going out of business. These opportunities could be a potential gold mine. Once you start looking you will develop 'dumpster eyes', learn the pattern when stores discard stuff, and even tell by how the bag feels or looks if it's worth checking out. Many times it's a hit or miss, some days you will find a ton of stuff and others nothing.

You can actually make money with all the goods you find. If you're good at woodworking, mechanics, or electronics you can fix up the furniture and electronics you find and resell them. If you find old aluminum, brass, or copper you can sell it for scrap. This construction site I was working at were the most wasteful people on Earth. They tossed away tons of lumber, plumbing, windows, doors, bricks, carpet, tiling, sheetrock, wiring, aluminum siding and studs, conduit, power sockets, furnishings, etc. Almost enough supplies for someone to build their own house!

Now it’s time for some words of warning in the area of potential enemies, safety, and legality. Enemies of dumpster divers include locked dumpsters, compactors, and anal pricks that insist on surrounding their dumpsters with razor wire and cameras or purposely dumping bleach or coffee grinds into food. Many dumpsters are locked not specifically to keep us out but to keep people from dumping stuff in. Compactors are annoying and usually used by corporate places but there's not much you can do about it just go to another place. However, if you’re feeling adventurous you could just clip the hydraulic lines on them. While thankfully rare, the anal pricks are people who just can't let anything go for free even if they're throwing it away. Their selfish attitude seems to be if

I can't sell it then nobody can have it, oh well fuck 'em. I know people who have clipped or glued locked dumpsters in retaliation. If you choose to do this that's up to you, however I'd just walk away and go to the next spot. As far as safety goes when diving watch sharp objects and broken glass. NEVER go inside compactors (you can get crushed to death) or medical waste/ hazardous material dumpsters (they contain biohazards). Legally, dumpster diving is perfectly legal. The Supreme Court in 1988 ruled anything in the trash is abandoned property that doesn't belong to anyone and is up for grabs. However, if the trash is on private property trespassing could be a problem. Use caution if it's in a gated area or if you must climb a fence. If someone sees you, say you're moving and looking for boxes or you're hungry and looking for food. If they get irate, avoid a confrontation simply say you're sorry and leave. You'll never win the argument plus they may decide to call the police. To avoid these complications do a recon of the dumpster first, check local laws, be discreet, be brief (under ten minutes), and don't make a mess. Not making a mess is **very** important because this is how good dumpsters get locked. Some poor underpaid worker will have to clean it, get pissed, and complain to the manager who will then lock it. Most workers can be quite helpful to you, don't alienate then by making extra work for them! Never ask permission to dive because if they say 'no' you can't dive, and you did that would be trespassing. Some professionals make a directory of the dumpsters indicating where it is, what's in it, if it's a one-off or continuing, best time to hit, and it's security (locked, guards, or cameras). Amusing but a bit excessive for me, it's a dumpster not a bank heist!

Pets

Obviously, the most frugal answer to this is not to have one. Then again, pet owners are less stressed out and have fewer heart attacks so maybe it cancels out. However if you already have one or want one do it according to your budget. Large dogs tend to be expensive while cats are cheaper and can be kept inside which is safer for them. Reptiles and fish can be expensive at first because they require special equipment but feeding them is cheap. Rodents by and far tend to be the cheapest. When buying food get quality, you'll save on vet bills in the long run. But instead of buying pet food in the supermarket you can make your own, find out how with at www.pet-grub.com. If you ever have to take your pet to the vet shop around for the best price. Check the vet college if there is one around. The price of vet medicine online is usually cheaper (just like people) check out www.petmarket.com. Talk with local organizations that can help you neuter your pet. Instead of buying kitty litter take a box line it with foil then newspaper and cover with shredded newspaper and crisp autumn leaves. Sprinkle baking soda in the box every once in a while to keep down odors. Do not buy toys for them, make your own like knotted socks, rope, towels, or old stuffed animals for dogs and pom-pom's and stuffed animals with catnip for cats.

www.ingramcontent.com/pod-product-compliance
Ingram Content Group UK Ltd.
Pitfield, Milton Keynes, MK11 3LW, UK
UKHW020241250726
13967UKWH00001B/500

9 781435 734500